FAMILY MATTERS

A Boy's Life in Depression-era Dorchester

James S. Doyle

Also by James S. Doyle

Not Above The Law: The Battles of Watergate Prosecutors Cox and Jaworsk

WITH LOVE
For Father John
Donald
Sister Mary (Lou)
Catherine (Cappy)
and Anne
In memory of Dad and Ma

We are all of us molded and remolded by those who have loved us.
And though that love may pass, we still remain the fruits of their work.
No love, no friendship can ever cross our paths without leaving some mark on us.
Francois Mauriac

Rear, John, Mary Lou, Donald Front, Anne, Jim, Catherine

Here is a photo of the six of us in Sunday best.

We used to go to Grove Hall or Franklin Park for Sunday afternoon picnics. I would sit on Dad's lap as the trolley car rocked along through the trees in the Cedar Grove Cemetery, wheels squealing, metal on metal. Tree leaves thwacked the window grate. The motorman stood in his dark uniform with bill cap and moved the wooden control knob in a tight arc—forward for speed, back to coast along, all the way back to stop. The wind was in my face, and my hands gripped the seat in front. It was the Great Depression. Everyone was poor and the world was a mess. The Doyle family of St. Mark Parish, Dorchester, was struggling like everyone else.

This is what I think I remember, or got from stories my brothers and sisters told me, about a family that mattered.

James S. Doyle

April 2015

Mary Cassie

She came from a bend in the road by the Margaree River.

Ma's birth certificate says Catherine Mary MacDonald, born March 12, 1897, in Southwest Margaree, Cape Breton Island, Nova Scotia. She was baptized in the Catholic church there the next day, March 13. The MacDonald farmhouse is at a rise in the road where the hills slope to bottom land along the river, cold and ribboned white in June, filled with fish pushing upstream from the Atlantic Ocean. When the sun is out and the wind is ruffling the tall grass, it's a place you don't want to leave. But like the harsh Scottish coasts where these people originated, the farms of Cape Breton could give out, and there were no jobs. So Mary Cassie MacDonald, (the family inverted her baptized name from the beginning), left for Boston when she was twenty-two. World War I was over, and Boston had jobs. It was a promising place to be, and she arrived just in time for the Roaring Twenties. In no time she was a domestic in the employ of a pedigreed Brookline family. Canadian girls with no brogues were much preferred to the Irish girls fresh off the boat, and "Catherine" was a good prospect—smart, well-mannered, with a good tenth-grade education. Violet Shepley Sweetser, her employer, was the striking wife of cotton merchant John Anderson Sweetser, Harvard graduate and naval officer during the war. Violet was the future matriarch of one of Boston's distinguished families. Catherine took to the Brahmins and their gentility far more than to the Irish stew pouring from the ships in the harbor. many desperate folks who had been coming to the States since the famine seventy-five years earlier, now a force in Boston city life and politics. Mrs. Sweetser, six years older than Catherine, had a baby, Julianne, and there were more to come. Catherine was soon essential to the family. Her role went from nanny for three baby girls to the family cook to Mrs. Sweetser's trusted housekeeper.

On Saturday nights, Catherine and her friends took the trolley to Rose Croix Hall in Roxbury where "down-easters," young people from Cape Breton, met and danced the night away to the sound of fiddles and a pounding piano, a singer or two, and maybe an accordion or guitar. The dancers stepped in lengthy sets that shook the hall for four hours or more with few breaks. There she met young Joe Doyle, a carpenter from Northeast Mabou, who worked for the Boston and Maine Railroad.

Donald Joseph Doyle was orphaned when he was five, the youngest of ten children. His twenty-year-old sister Ellen and her husband kept the family together and ran a grist mill on the family farm. Joe did chores and got no schooling. He helped with the mill until he was fourteen, then joined construction teams and learned carpentry. He could not read or write, and was shy. His left eye was turned, so it seemed like he didn't look people directly in the face.

When they met, Joe was twenty-eight and Catherine, twenty-two. Four years later, on October 8, 1924, they were married in St. Lawrence Catholic Church, Brookline, by Rev. Thomas F. McManus. And though Catherine would soon be pregnant and giving notice, the Sweetsers and a few of their friends who loved her would remain in her life.

Boston in 1924 was rich and well-mannered at the top and rowdy further down where the immigrants were gaining a foothold. Its Yankee politics were like those of ex-Governor Calvin Coolidge, who had broken the Boston Police strike five years before and parlayed that into a landslide second term, then to the vice presidency, and the presidency upon the death of Warren G. Harding. Harding's and Coolidge's clueless attitudes were in contrast to Boston's realities. Still the Brahmins, sober financiers, sought to stay in charge, to remain as learned, but also as arrogant and provincial, as when Oliver Wendell Holmes called the city the hub of the universe seventy years earlier. They clung to the idea that whatever was worthy in commercial and intellectual life began not far from Beacon Hill, Harvard, MIT, and the Boston Athenaeum.

But the politics of Boston had changed. Irish Catholics had been flooding the area for decades, and a Protestant backlash against the papists and against immigration itself was growing. Working people everywhere were struggling, shaking their heads. Harding was too inept to face the freebooting corruption around him, and Coolidge was smug, happy to let the good times roll apparently as smoothly as his own fake but solemn truisms: "The business of America is business." "The man who builds a factory builds a temple." Biology, he said, meant "divergent people will not blend." He fiddled, left everything alone, and Rome slowly burned.

Prohibition and its gangsters were literally raising hell across our cities, along with racial and ethnic strife. The inequality was ominous. Much of rural America was weaker even than the farms in Cape Breton. The Ku Klux Klan was resurgent. But the country was spurting postwar growth—half the world's manufacture was from the United States. New Fords were rolling off the Highland Park assembly line, every third home owned a radio, and indoor plumbing was almost ordinary. Telephones were the coming thing. Optimism reigned alongside the dance marathons, the flappers, and the bathtub gin.

If you were in love and had a steady job, things were not bad for the white working man. On their wedding day Joe and Catherine moved into a rented duplex at 22A Melbourne Street in Dorchester, once a sprawling town that extended south to Rhode Island, now sliced off and annexed to Boston, much smaller than it was but still dwarfing in size the other Boston suburbs. It was the place for striving blue- and white-collar families. The Doyle flat was across from a ball field and a block from the modern subway system to downtown. The unique made-in-Boston "three-deckers" and duplexes were spreading across these new neighborhoods, empowering a new class of owners who lived in one flat and paid the mortgage by renting the rest of the house. This had been out of reach for the working class who were crammed into the tenements in Roxbury and the South End. It was further away, beyond South

Boston, and by the 1920s, there were flourishing parishes where the Catholic diocese built imposing churches and schools and communities for the immigrant church in America.

Catherine and Joe were young and optimistic and looking forward. A beautiful, healthy boy was born on July 15, 1925, but something quickly went wrong. He wasn't thriving, not holding down any food. He was baptized at home as Donald Joseph Doyle Junior, then taken to Boston City Hospital, one of the best hospitals in the country. On July 31 he died. My sister Catherine (Cappy), who trained as a nurse at City twenty-five years later, believes from the symptoms that the baby died of pyloric stenosis, a thickening of the muscle surrounding the outlet of the stomach. The symptoms usually start a week after birth with projectile vomiting, then loss of weight, then dehydration. Today, an ultrasound or other scan would pick up the condition, and surgeons would open up the passageway. But in 1925, my parents were not told that their new baby starved to death or why. My father used to recall the assurances a doctor gave them when they brought the baby to the hospital. They were reeling—incredulous—when a few days later, they were told the baby died of "jaundice".

The next baby came seventeen months later, on January 11, 1927. They named this second son John Lawrence, and the picture of Mary Cassie, age twenty-nine, holding John Lawrence in her lap shows a beautiful, smiling young woman, her face serene. John would be the son who led the way, who from childhood took on the responsibilities and met all the demands and expectations of the oldest son in a big Catholic family. What pressures he felt, what obligations, I can only guess, but they were great. He was a protective and dutiful brother as the family grew, and then as a parish priest he was caring and conscientious. He left for the "missions" as soon as he was permitted: first in Utah, then for thirty-five years among the poorest people of Bolivia, always ending up with the poorest of the poor. He spent his life quietly angry at poverty, at injustice, at neglect of human beings—and converted that anger into a spiritual quest that made him a holy man who helped people and was loved for it.

After John came Donald Justin, Mary Louise, Catherine Patricia, and Anne Theresa, each separated by fourteen to seventeen months. I was born three years after Anne, with the likelihood that there was a miscarried pregnancy between us. Ma gave birth to me on June 18, 1935, and after me there were two more pregnancies. Cecelia died at birth in September 1938, and then some time later, a stillborn male fetus was delivered at Lying-In--Ma's tenth.

Engagement, Brookline 1924

2

Joe

Mabou is some fifty miles south of Margaree--a pretty inlet town on the west coast where two branches of the Mabou River meet and meander out to the Gulf of St. Lawrence. It is surrounded by low mountains dotted with old coal mines that were thriving when Donald Joseph Doyle was born there on February 4, 1892, the youngest of ten.

The mines gave out, but the fertile farmland is still there, along with a small fleet of picture-perfect lobster boats and some fancy pubs and restaurants, catering to the tourists who come to hear the fiddlers (including the world-famous Rankin family) and hope to peek at the summer residents from the New York music world (composer Philip Glass, filmmaker Robert Frank, others), or the writers from Toronto, retired Canadian politicians from Ottawa, and others who find Cape Breton a haven.

Dad's father, James Doyle, died when Dad was one. His mother, Mary Beaton Doyle, died when he was five, and his oldest sister Ellen, who was twenty and married, was left to care for him. With almost no schooling, he left home in his early teens. The Inverness and Richmond Railway had opened in 1901 to connect the mines to wharves in Mabou and Port Hastings, and he may have started there. He helped build Canada's railroads, then the bridge over Halifax Harbor where he worked in a pressurized diving bell, sometimes getting the bends when he surfaced. He was smart, quiet, good-looking, and successful. Folks say he was among the first in Mabou to own a motorcar.

I can't remember many stories Dad told of his youth, but one was of the beavers whose dams would be dynamited to make way for the tracks, and by the next day or two, new beaver dams were flooding the same place. He told of visiting a friend's farm and being greeted by a mean-looking, charging dog. Dad waited until the dog was almost upon him and swung his boot, connecting square under the animal's chin. The dog flipped, ass over teakettle, righted itself, and raced off, tail between its legs. Dad remembered that.

After World War I, he joined the parade of Cape Bretoners who traveled south across Nova Scotia and New Brunswick to the American border crossing at Calais, Maine, then on to Boston where there were jobs. He would have been eighteen or nineteen, and he cut quite a figure. A formal picture taken around the time of his marriage shows him seated in an armchair in a fitted dark suit, a starched white shirt and dark-patterned necktie, his big right hand closed and resting lightly against his tilted face, his big left hand resting on his knee and holding a folded magazine. He has on round glasses with tortoise-shell frames, a sharp-angled face, full lips, a prominent nose, high forehead, and a full head of dark hair slightly parted on the left side. He could be an author friend of Scott Fitzgerald's or a banker who palled around with Joseph P. Kennedy.

All his life he could barely read or write, but he figured out signs, learned the subway stops, and read comic strips. On Sundays, he delighted in reading with us "Nancy" by Ernie Bushmiller in the *Sunday Globe*. It was a struggle, even after successful years in Boston where he ran the mill room at Summerfield's Furniture Company, joined the St. Vincent DePaul Society helping the poorest families at St. Mark, ushered every week at the 7:00 a.m. Sunday Mass in a suit with vest, starched white shirt, and proper necktie. He was one of the men who kept St. Mark running, building add-ons to the church and school, finishing altars, handcrafting the polished wooden signals used by the nuns to prompt us kids to stand or sit. He conscientiously raised the six of us, and mourned the four who didn't survive. My mother was worn out by it all, subject to moods. My father was worn out as well, but except for a few collapses that landed him in the hospital (undiagnosed heart attack, simple exhaustion), he kept on.

His gift was working wood. He made an elaborate three-story parking garage with ramps for cars and trucks to traverse, guided by little hands. It was gone by the time I arrived; gone but well remembered.

When I was an errant preteen, Dad used to take me on jobs in the parish. Once it was to the convent across from our house where he was spiffing up the altar with new wooden adornments as a favor to the sacristan, Sister Gertrude Clair. She taught fifth-grade boys, and I had her that year. That very day in class, "Two-gun Gertie" had returned from a comfort call and walked in to catch me cocking a ruler as if it were a spear and launching it toward the blackboard. She was not about to repay my father with heartbreak, so she said nothing about the incident. I don't think Dad was aware of the terror in my soul that evening.

He took me to the new parish hall where he was supervising the interior finishing, and I watched as he boxed in the fuse panels or installed baseboard. He took me to the nicer neighborhoods where he was building a porch or finishing a basement. I handed him tools but never got the hang of any of them. I listened to him whistle under his breath. We shared sandwiches from home. We almost never talked, but we were comfortable. I loved being with him.

We went to Malibu Beach and changed together in the bath house. Every time we passed the hot dog stand, I would ask for one. Every time he would say, "I wouldn't give a nickel for a wheelbarrow full of them." He put together a bicycle for me out of parts, including chrome fenders. He took me looking for school clothes—sometimes used but mostly new—and always said not to tell Ma what the price was.

My children now have the pine study table he made for me when I was in high school, with its inlaid laminated surface, thin clean legs, drawer with a chrome pull handle. When I was a naval officer, Dad made a walnut-veneer cabinet to contain my hi-fi audio equipment and record turntable, as well as a matching walnut cabinet with slots for LP recordings.

With financial help from my employer, *The Boston Globe*, my wife Ann and I bought a home when we moved to the Washington area. It was a fixer-upper. Dad visited, and we went together to Hechinger's ("The store for Harry Homeowner"), where I watched him pick out what I needed. The clerk, toothpick between lips, brought forth a piece of lumber. Dad, that meek man, held it in his grip, measured it with his eyes, walked past the clerk to the vertical stacks of lumber in back, and started hefting one piece after another, his muscular arms sorting, gathering. When he was finished, the clerk wrote up the order without a word. I got the car and brought it around to the loading platform.

I have some of Dad's tools—saws with hand-carved handles, a solid toolbox that he carried on his shoulder through the South End. I remember accompanying him once as he applied for assembly line carpentry jobs after World War II when Summerfield's Furniture Co. let him go. There's other stuff—planes, blades, boxes of files each in a slot. There's a Stanley No. 76 tool with two handles on either side of a circular hole and a small chisel blade protruding that looks like you might use it to finish a keyhole. I can't do much with them, but I like to hold them in my hand.

My neighborhood hardware is a narrow little store with crowded aisles and long lines at the cashier. If the line is too long when I go there to pick up fertilizer or lawn seed or leaf bags, I wait instead by heading for the row of bright blue slide-out trays, long and slim, that runs from the floor to above eye level. The signs on each tray mean little to me: *¼ in. sheet metal, 2 in. stove bolts, machine screws, push nuts, knurled nuts, concrete screws, gate hooks, clevis pins.* At intervals along this aisle, there are hand-painted signs that say: "Cashier will need prices," meaning that this is an honor system. Even customers who are used to cheating about bigger things in life are expected to write the true price per item as they slip the hardware into tiny paper bags. I remember Dad sliding out these trays, picking up a single screw, and turning it over in his calloused hand, fingering the ridges, and looking through his bifocals for something—a fault of some kind, or a sign of structural integrity.

Catherine, Mary Lou, Anne, Ma

3

Margaree

August 30, 1933. On December 2, 1930, we got a new sister for Mary Lou. Had our dear nurse Miss Donnelly, also Dr. Cyril M. Lydon who, through good fortune, has never failed us. Catherine Patricia is now near three years old and has another sister Anne, born March 1, 1932. She is now one year and a half, so we'll have to get some pictures of them all in our book to complete it.

Mother has been sick a lot since those two were born, and her father died.

Catherine Doyle in the Family Baby Book

The country and the world became poorer and more ugly on October 29, 1929—two months after Mary Lou was born. Wall Street crashed, and the world economy was smashed by exactly the wrong policies of austerity, retrenchment, and protection of the richest at the expense of the poorest. The United States, Canada, and Europe ended the exuberant march toward better times.

By early 1932 when Anne came, 13 million American workers—one in four—were without jobs. The country still needed radios and telephones, electricity and roads, and indoor plumbing, but the market just quit. Crops rotted in the fields. Farmers dumped life-giving gallons of fresh milk across highways to protest collapsed prices. People ate starch or weeds or dirt, and in the cities, garbage. Forty million Americans, including most blacks and Indians and many arriving immigrants, were subsisting below what the government called the minimum subsistence level.

Dad was working steadily and that was a triumph in those times. The family had moved one street over to 41 Samoset Street (across from St. Mark Parish School), where Dad and Ma could afford the second floor and the attic for their steadily growing number of babies. They were lucky with that steady paycheck, but life was getting harder.

In 1934, Ma was thirty-seven years old—exhausted, depressed, and homesick. In late spring, she headed back to Cape Breton with her five children to try to restore her health and spirits. She had just lost a baby and longed to see her mother. She had lived in Boston for fifteen years and had been married for ten. Her father, James MacDonald, had died in 1930, but she hadn't made it home for his funeral. And this trip would be the last time she would see Catherine Gillis MacDonald, her mother.

Northwest Margaree. The land firm and rich to the till in late spring, the hay thick and green; and thousands of herring—"gaspereau"—swimming up the Margaree River to where they were born. Ma's brother Jack dammed the stream along the intervale and netted the fish, salted them, and took them to market. The herring were a dependable catch when the crops failed. Because Catholics ate fish on Friday, in Boston they were called "mackerel snappers," Cape Bretoners were called "herring chokers."

My brothers and sisters often talked about that summer of 1934. Young Uncle Jack enlisted seven-year-old John and six-year-old Donald to net the spawning herring as they struggled up the spillway, filling barrel after barrel. Many, many years later, I visited Uncle Jack at that farm, and he drove me down the slope from the farmhouse to the intervale, and I could imagine my brothers waking up fifty years earlier in that farmhouse, racing to dress and eat and head out on the wagon with Jack, across the fields of tall grass, drying in the early morning sun, then perched atop the hay wagon as Jack and his neighbors packed in the bales and the boys manhandled them into place, while my three sisters played together near the farmhouse.

Friends in Boston always called my mother Catherine, but back home, she was Mary Cassie. She and her mother busied themselves in the farmhouse, talking and cooking as neighbors came along the road, their shoes stained by the red earth, and stopped to visit and see the Doyle children. In the evening, my mother would sit on a little porch and look over the fields at the pewter sky and the tranquil meander of the Margaree, and know why her father and her mother and her brother Jack had each tried Boston but returned.

As her burdens grew, Mary Cassie suffered from depression brought on by exhaustion, poverty, too many pregnancies, rage. The warning of her obstetrician could not be heeded when my parents knew birth control as a sin, if they knew anything about it. (When I was a young married man, my father and I were talking once and he said to me, "We knew nothing when we married.") My father didn't know how to protect my mother, his marriage, or his children, when it came to sexuality.

Catherine and her children had a wonderful summer in Margaree, one they would remember throughout their long lives. They were back home by September, in time for school. And within a few months, Catherine was pregnant again, with me.

4

James Stephen

February 18, 1936. It is near three years since we wrote any history of our family. James Stephen who was born last June is now six months old and dearer than any of them if that is possible. He came on Tuesday, as did all the other children.

Anne was run over by an auto July twenty-seventh and was in the hospital until October first. When she came home, Mary Lou and Catherine were in the hospital with scarlet fever. Donald had it in April, so we had a tedious summer and fall.

Dad has had more or less rest from his stomach trouble, thank heavens.

Catherine Doyle in the Baby Book

Having an eighth child was too much in a worldwide economic depression, when two earlier babies had died and life was a daily struggle. I was the happy beneficiary of two earnest farm kids unaware of how to avoid having babies even if it hadn't been against their religion. They did know how to endure hard times though, and that is what they faced together: exhaustion, terrifying illnesses, little money or chance of escaping the downward spiral of many children and not many resources—emotional, physical, or financial—with which to care for those children.

It was a difficult pregnancy from the outset. Catherine would take the subway downtown to a clinic at the Boston Lying-In Hospital, which offered excellent obstetrical care free. According to my nurse-sister Cappy, the chief of obstetrics at Lying-In, who had treated Ma in the past, now told her he would not treat her. In frustration, he handed her off to a staff doctor because she had ignored his repeated warnings to avoid further pregnancies. And then late in the pregnancy, in April 1935, my brother Donald, then seven, contracted scarlet fever. It was a terrifying illness, a highly infectious type of streptococcus that has since been eradicated by antibiotics. It usually began with a sore throat and headache like an ordinary cold. Then came a puffy face, a strawberry tongue, a nasty red rash, and a fever that might rise to 105 degrees. In many cases, the rash would fade after four or five days, and skin would peel off the child in large wafers. Deadly complications—pneumonia, rheumatic fever, deep tissue infections—often followed. Women exposed during pregnancy were vulnerable.

In those days, Boston was a pioneering center for treating infectious diseases. Donald was taken to the Boston City Hospital's South Department, a famous isolation ward for children. While there, he could have no visitors and no contact with his family. There was a courtyard under balcony windows where family members came to wave to their terrified kids looking down from above. Donald remembers being told by a nurse that his father was in the courtyard. When he ran to the balcony he saw only the distant forms of Dad and John, walking away. They had been there in the cold, waiting for a long time. He yelled to them but it was no use. The physical scars of his illness went away, but not that painful memory.

Ma escaped scarlet fever. I was born on the eighteenth of June, preceded by a furious rainstorm. The next morning's *Boston Globe* reported on the lives and commerce and graduation ceremonies disrupted by that storm.

I was delivered by Dr. Lydon and his new nurse, Miss Lenihan, in the front bedroom of the duplex at 41 Samoset Street in Dorchester. I am the youngest of the six children who lived. People weren't having many babies during the Great Depression, and Ma must have missed the comfort and calm of the Sweetser house in Brookline. She was deeply depressed by the time I arrived. I was a healthy baby, and that was a good thing for me at least, but the added burden on Ma was not good.

One month later, before Ma had a chance to regain strength, she found herself one Saturday, standing in the street in front of our duplex, looking at the tiny, terrified face and broken body of Anne, her youngest daughter. Ma had been inside resting with me. John was in the backyard minding the others when Lamporelli the iceman parked his truck across the street. John and Donald raced from the backyard and across the busy street to scoop up shavings as Mr. Lamporelli chipped a thirty-pound block for our icebox.

Nobody noticed three-year-old Anne running across the street to join her brothers. A passing auto smacked her down, smashing her leg. The driver was a local man—his brother was the then radio voice of the Red Sox. He put Anne in his car and drove to City Hospital. Anne was terrified, not at all comforted by the smiling aide who told her they were going to take her picture as she was wheeled into the X ray room. Anne's memories of this hospital stay are troubled ones, and she is openly bitter that she remembers no visitors and no nurturing. Her leg was in traction above her prone body one day when a nurse came by and saw Anne had wet herself. The nurse slapped her across the face. There is a haunting school portrait of Anne taken later. The teacher lined her up with the other kindergarteners and announced they were going to have their picture taken. The result shows Anne staring into the lens, terror in her eyes, the color drained from her face, expecting to be hurt again.

Anne was still in the hospital in October when first Catherine and then Mary Lou came down with scarlet fever. Cappy remembers:

I was four, Lou was five. Nothing was told to us. We were upstairs at 41 Samoset Street in one of the bedrooms, and two men came up with what I will call horse blankets. They wrapped us up mummy style in them, and carried us downstairs. Ma, Dad—nobody told us anything. You know? Nothing was told to us. And you know we never had a car, and how often were we in a car? It was after dark, and they took us down out of the house and put us in an ambulance and away we went.

...And then we get into the hospital, and of course it's South Department because it was an infectious disease. South Department was a whole different ball of wax. It was across the street from main City Hospital, and of course, what did we know? I was only a baby. So they took us in there and somebody picked us up. The next thing I knew, some guy rolled me inside a mattress and carried me—inside the mattress that was still rolled around me—and dropped me in a crib. You know, with the mattress going the opposite way, and there I lay, just terrified with all these lights on, and I didn't know...I don't think Lou was right there with me at that time. So there I lay rolled up in this mattress, not knowing what in the name of God was going on. I didn't even know I was sick. And so I laid there for a while. Finally somebody must have come, because that's the end of that particular memory.

Later on we were put in iron cribs, and for a while we were side by side. But then, after a day or so, they moved Lou away from me. She was put in another area. It was a big, round, open ward. When I went back as a student nurse and saw those wards—I mean, it was like a flashback. Same ward. And I remembered—and I can tell you this for a fact—the head nurse on the ward we were in. She ended up head of the Nursing Arts Department where the students were trained. And I knew it was her: Dolena MacGinniss.

It was Halloween, and we were getting better. And then they brought into the ward a dummy, dressed up like a witch. I was terrified, absolutely. Lou was somewhere across the room from me, and I didn't know what was happening to her or where she was, and they had put this thing in the middle of the room. At night, they would roll it out and put it up against a frosted-panel side door, and I would lay and look at the shadow of that thing in terror—sheer terror! I have the clearest memories of that.

Then I also got an infected finger. I tore a hangnail, and they had to call a surgeon. I know it was a surgeon because he was a doctor who didn't belong there, and he came over, and he dressed and treated the finger.

I don't know how many weeks we were there, but I know it was a long time. I didn't know what home was. I thought we would never go back. The day Mom came to pick us up, the young student nurse bathed and dressed me, and I didn't know where, why, or what was going on. I remember the young nurse must have been yelled at because she was crying. I started crying when I saw that, because I didn't know what was coming. Then I was taken to a waiting room, and Lou was there. And then she ran across the room to this woman. The woman was Ma. I didn't know her. I had no idea who that woman was.

They say God doesn't give you more than you can handle, but my mother got a bit too much. Three years after me, she carried a little girl baby full term. She was to be Jane, named after an aunt. But this baby had no strength and no capacity, and she died almost immediately. The hospital chaplain baptized her as she slipped away and he named her Cecilia after his mother. That's the way her death certificate reads, but we call her Jane. There was a tenth pregnancy, a stillborn male baby, some years later.

Her body spent, her soul depleted, anger took over. Ma lashed out at small things and blamed whoever was nearby. Every member of the family paid the price. As the baby in this big, struggling brood, I was lucky to be alive and cared for by seven people who loved me. But I was daily witness to my mother losing control and becoming more and more depressed and angry. I learned good and bad things that stay with me.

Ma was in the hospital, pregnant with baby Jane, on September 21, 1938, when the Great New England Hurricane of 1938 slammed into Long Island, New York, and kept coming. It smashed through Connecticut, then Rhode Island, Cape Cod, the South Shore, Boston, and north all the way to the Maritime Provinces. It came without much advance word from the weather man. The deaths and damage were greater by far than those of the

Chicago fire of 1871 or the San Francisco earthquake and fire of 1906. In New England, there were 680 deaths. Forty-five hundred buildings were destroyed, and thirteen thousand more damaged. A million trees were down. Power was out for days. It took a week to restore railroad service between New York and Boston.

Aunt Sadie, a sister of Dad, had come from her North Shore home to take care of us. She was warm and calm, singing under her breath mornings as she dry-mopped the kitchen floor. My mother was having a difficult pregnancy, and the doctor was scolding her that she was forty-one, neither young nor healthy enough to have more children. Her blood pressure was through the roof.

I have this gauzy image—the storm is part of family history—of standing at the living room window on the second floor of our duplex, the sky black, wind thrashing about. Dad was at Summerfield's, John and Donald probably at Connolly's Market, Catherine, seven, and Anne, six, were home. Mary Lou, just nine, was outside with Mary Mulligan, both sitting on the sidewalk with their backs against a swaying tree, feeling the wind and the tree moving against them. Neighbors yelled at them to get away from the tree and go home. Lou came home and watched with us from the parlor; Aunt Sadie led me away from the window. I can hear the crack of huge branches and the explosion of an uprooted trunk buckling the street, and feel the house tremble.

When it was over, the street was clogged with trunks and branches, and as quiet as the dawn after a heavy snow. People opened the side-by-side front doors of their duplexes or came down from the three-deckers to gape at the lines of broken trees. The houses were depression-weary with flaking paint and struggling lawns and empty window boxes, but they were standing. On our block of Samoset Street most trees were down, the street was pockmarked with holes, and some of the porches were smashed. But the houses, as close together as they were, survived.

"Potatohead" Murphy, the short, bald, blinking man who owned the three-decker at 33 Samoset, stood guard in front, as he often did on weekends to keep us from using his front steps for a game of stoopball or chalking his sidewalk. In front of number 48, Shurgrue's, a fire truck stood, its crew using ropes to stabilize a leaning tree that threatened the house. All the bigger kids were out on the street, over their fears, full of excited energy.

My father, coming home from work that day, must have looked down the street where we lived, saw the destruction and the branches of a broken tree covering the front of our duplex, and asked himself if his children were safe. They were. (Not long after that, I lined up with my brothers and sisters in front of the little white coffin for newborn Jane at Doran's Funeral Home, as we said the rosary.)

———

It was a long time before road crews came to resurface Samoset Street and put in curbs. Muscled men swung pickaxes, hefted shovels, and held slow conferences on warm days. The older kids were in school and the younger ones at home. I stood there alone on the sidewalk, watching. I talked to the crew, asked questions, and wandered around making myself part of the project. There are no photographs, but I picture a ruddy-cheeked four-year-old, probably in knickers and a too-big white shirt with the sleeves rolled up and tiny arms poking out. I wore the clothes that came to my house through the mail, big parcel post boxes from Mrs. Sweetser.

I would be up early each day, there with Ma and Dad in the chilly kitchen, crammed in the handmade high chair, eating oatmeal. Dad, back from the cellar with a tank of white gas, would start the big, black, cast-iron woodstove that had been fitted with oil burners. Ma would make a pot of tea. They would talk together in the Gaelic of Cape Breton Island, laugh at a joke-- or something I said. (The family lore is that often it was the demand, "Cook a egg for me!"). Ma would add milk to the tea, pour some of it into a brown pint whiskey bottle, and put the bottle into a brown paper sack with Dad's sandwiches. He then carried his lunch down the steep back stairs and up the hill to the rapid transit train at Shawmut Station, to Kendall Square and Summerfield's Furniture Company. At noon he would turn off the rotary saws and other machines in the mill room, put the whiskey bottle in a glue pot, heat the tea, and eat the sandwiches, six days a week.

Anne and I slept with Ma and Dad in the front room of the third-floor attic, me in an oversized crib and Anne in a bed Dad had made. My brothers and sisters slept in the other attic room—John and Donald in one bed, and Lou and Cappy in another. The ceiling sloped, and the beds were tucked under the low walls. You could look above your head and see a smear where someone had swatted a mosquito, red splotch on the dingy white.

I used to imagine that my high-walled crib was the back of a truck, and I was aboard for a warm, safe ride. I remember nightmares—not dreams with people in them but scary movements and dark colors—and Dad would stand above me and rub my face and soothe me. One night I awakened to a noise and from the upward glow of a streetlamp, I could see Dad at the window looking down. Ma lay on the bed, telling Dad to come away from the window. In a slow whisper she was saying, *"Eus, Eus, Eus"*—the Gaelic word for *Jesus*.

I could hear rough voices, men god-damning a neighbor who owned a shiny black sedan that he chauffeured to take people on special occasions for business or weddings. (Once he took Ma and the girls to a Sweetser wedding in Brookline.) Now men were roughing him up, playing a drunken, vicious version of *Red Rover, Red Rover, send Gaffney over.* I learned later that one group would beat him and then send him to another, laughing like hyenas, howls fed by whiskey. My father opened the attic window and tried to shout in his soft voice: "Break it up! The police have been called!" But the police hadn't been called. We had no telephone, the other houses were dark and silent including next door where lived a Boston policeman with rowdy sons. He had a telephone and knew the score. Was this a union fight or was the chauffer involved with shady characters? I don't know.

My life was filled with terrors, large and small.

—

Each morning after Dad left for work, one after another we used the bathroom and flushed the toilet with the twice-used bath and laundry water that was in buckets next to the toilet bowl. To my mother, this was saving water as one would do on a farm where every gallon had to be lugged from a failing well. To us, it was a family secret of which I was ashamed. My brothers and sisters washed and dressed and straggled down the stairs to breakfast in the dim, noisy kitchen.

Ma was friendly but steered clear of the neighbors except at church and Ladies Sodality. We didn't gossip about others because we were our own secret—the house always messy, Ma tearing into us. Plus the landlords, the Nesdale family who lived in a single-family house at the end of Samoset, were right there to observe us. Now and then, Mrs. Nesdale would confront Ma or leave her a note complaining about the water bill, and my mother would tell her how conscientious we were about that. Ma worried that we would be evicted.

She felt superior to our neighbors. They all read the *Globe* or the *Post,* the Democratic paper. We were diehard Roosevelt Democrats like everyone else, but Ma got *The Boston Herald*—I guess because she was used to it from her Brookline days. I grew up on *Herald* columnists. They wrote well, but many were Yankees with a permanent bone to pick with Irish politicians. The *Herald* was always after Mayor (or Congressman or Governor or inmate) James Michael Curley, and found his flamboyant mischief a source for constant journalistic ire. My mother would read about his antics and sum it up: "The dirty Irish!"

John and Donald had jobs to go to before starting the school day. Mary Lou would lift me from the high chair and help me dress each morning. Perhaps I should have been dressing myself at four, but Lou seldom said what I heard from others: *Stop being a baby.*

My three sisters would be off to join the orderly lines of girls and boys waiting in the yard of St. Mark Parish School, across the street. I would walk past the schoolyard to the top of the hill where drivers sat in their dump trucks, cigarettes pointing out from their mouths, their truck beds tilting to unload dirt and gravel.

I can see this big fellow in a brown leather jacket, leaning on a shovel, asking my name.

"James Stephen Doyle."

"Glory be to God, what a big name."

He sets aside his shovel, lifts me above his head, and swings me down. I get a queasy, panicky feeling deep in my stomach and hide my fear. I want to be part of this, away from the house.

During the summer I hung around with the kids who had already started at St. Mark School. We roamed the block, rebounding rubber balls off the stoops into the pockmarked street, and watched the big kids play hearts or poker until they shooed us away because they were going to play for money. We teased Mr. Lamporelli the ice man, Mr. Hall the driver of the Happy Home Bakery truck, and Eddie Moloney of the Whiting's Milk wagon, to take us along for a block or two. Never mind the little sign affixed to the cab that said no riders.

When school started, I walked the neighborhood alone, looking for companions, big or small. There was Father Augustus Dalton, who strolled by often enough but was always busy and, though a friend of my family, not good for more than a brief conversation. (I did earn his admiration when the neighborhood German Shepherd barked at him and I admonished "Rippy, stop that! He's a priest!" John tells of the time Dad went to confession to Fr. Dalton and after hearing Dad's sins Father Dalton said, *Joe, how's the battleaxe?*)

At the end of the block, the frail and white-bearded "gumdrop man" sat in his wheelchair, wrapped in blankets, soaking in the sun. He couldn't speak, and in any case, my sisters, who had named him, frightened me away. He kept a bag of candy in his lap and would summon children up to receive some. Once Anne and Cappy had ventured up on the man's porch and taken a few gumdrops and then ran home. I discovered them, two shadowy figures in the front stairwell, backs leaning against the shut door. They threw the candy away.

I walked Samoset Street alone. I watched the mailman come and go, his leather bag burdened with letters. He'd make his way down Samoset Street and then back to the steel pickup box that he unlocked with a key dangling from a chain, and there would be envelopes tied neatly in bundles. He'd fill the leather pouch and set out again along his route. I decided I wanted to be the mailman. I told Dad, and he made a frame out of thin strips of wood, stretched black oilcloth around the frame, stenciled US MAIL in white paint on the top flap, and tacked a shoulder strap onto the sides. Ma gave me the enclosures from the electric bill and a few other scraps to carry in the bag, and soon I expanded my ambitions.

I intercepted the official mailman and accepted his letters for the Doyles. I took one or two of the pieces—official-looking, typed envelopes—and put them in my own mail pouch. Then I delivered them to the US Post Office mailbox right next to the one the mailman opened. When this seemed to work well, I expanded. There was a space by the back stairs where Ma kept old letters--shopping bags spilling over with mail from Canada, letters from Ma's mother, from Aunt Agnes, Aunt Jane, Mary Gillis, Dad's brother in Halifax and Ma's sister in Saskatchewan. Each had a small square hole in the right-hand corner of the envelope where the Canadian stamp had been removed, interrupting the wavy cancellation mark. I took three or four letters several times a day for several days, placed them in my pouch, carried them up the hill, reached up, and pulled down the big handle. Then I slid the letters one by one into the mailbox.

The United States postal inspector made a special visit to deliver these letters to Ma. He had a badge in a wallet. He was courteous, and once the mystery was solved, he was friendly and reassuring. Dad and Ma were citizens, and yet the postal inspector struck the fear of God into my mother, and made her furious at my father for making me a mailbag..

I had to give up the mailbag and spend more time in the house I had come to dislike, with a mother who was unpredictable. Mornings I would watch the kids lining up in the schoolyard, walk to the top of the hill, then race back down the sidewalk, angling into the alley at 41, and up the steep back stairs. I'd catch the unfriendly smells of homemade lye soap, greens overcooking on the stove though it was hours before dinner; dirty water in the sink. I'd see the disarray of the back hall, the mess of old food and newspaper clippings and other papers on the kitchen table. My mother would be there, still in her nightdress, standing over the stove, talking to herself.

One day I was still in my pajamas, sitting against the wall on the kitchen bench while Ma worked at the stove. Dad always got her the latest in utensils, and she had a new "double-boiler" that she hadn't quite gotten the hang of. Suddenly it erupted—the cover flew off, and a stream of scalding liquid hit Ma full in the face. She was blinded and badly hurt, but she didn't tell me to run and get help or ask a neighbor who had a phone to call for help. Instead, she sent me upstairs to the bathroom and told me to bring her the Unguentine. I tried to find the tube she wanted, but there were several tubes, among them Unguentine, a cream for burns, but others like Bengay for muscle aches that would have done further damage to her burns. I had no idea what I was doing. Ma stayed calm, but she was badly hurt. I don't remember much about that day except that nobody came to our help until the girls and maybe my brothers got home. After a while, Ma's face mostly cleared up, but she had a nasty lump on her right shoulder for a long, long time; maybe forever.

Most days were better than that. I have fond memories of coming home for lunch. At noon Ma would turn on the radio, and a voice named Ted Collins would say: "It's high noon in New York and time for Kate Smith!" And then Ted and Kate would talk about life. It was very interesting.

—

When the road gang showed up to repave Samoset Street, I spent hours watching. They greeted me in the morning. They called me "James Stephen" and asked how I was and what I had been up to and what was on my mind. There was something about the company of those men and the size of the job that has stayed with me. At the time, it was all I talked about. I talked about the men at supper, naming each by his familiar clothes: the leather-jacket man, the red-jacket man, the blue-jacket man. I knew what they carried in their lunch pails and what feats of strength they accomplished with their pickaxes, air hammers, broad backs, and big muscles. To me they were more than a road gang happy to have work. And I was as much a part of them as Donald and John were part of the working world at Connolly's Market or the Golden Ring Donut Shop. The crew could count on me to be there every morning, standing on the sidewalk, watching, pacing, asking, "what's that for?" and telling of my latest hike or bike ride with my brother John.

In the late afternoon, I would walk the few blocks to Shawmut Station along with one or more of my sisters and wait on the upper level by the change booth for the arrival of the rapid transit train. We would hear a roar, a rush of wind up the stairwells, the sound of the train doors snapping open, and then we'd see the slowly bobbing heads of fathers struggling up the stairs, fatigue on their faces and stiffness in their legs. Eventually one would be Joe Doyle with the turned eye and soft voice and shy manner. We kids would wait and then fall in next to him, walking quietly through the swinging station doors and down the street. There were no hugs or kisses and not much talk. Dad's reticence and his constant struggle with language set the tone. But at supper, in the safe privacy of the duplex, the accumulation of the day's tensions at school and at work might mushroom into discord, incoherence, squabbles. Ma was back and forth from the stove, speaking to Dad in Gaelic.

Ma coped despite her short temper and unpredictable ways. Sometimes she would take to the bed in the front bedroom downstairs with migraine headaches, and the house would get quiet, but she would be moaning and shouting and screaming, which is not what happens when you have a migraine and you just want your head to stop hurting. You want it dark and quiet.

One summer when I was five or six, she and I went on the subway train to Charles Street Station and walked to the Hatch Shell on the Charles River looking across to the Cambridge shore. It was before sunset, and Ma got herself a chair in the audience for ten cents. She told me to stay by the concert ground and when the music ended, to meet her under a lamppost she pointed out. I got along fine, watching the crowd and listening to Arthur Fiedler and the Boston Pops Orchestra. But when the concert ended and the people started streaming along the esplanade, I went to the designated lamppost—and the light was out! It seemed all shadows. So I walked along to the next lamppost where it was well lit. I figured Ma would see me there. It was a while before she came. She walked up to me and smacked me hard in the face with her open hand! I was reeling—stunned, hurt, and shamed before the crowd of onlookers. She hustled me to the subway station, and all the way home as we sat together in the swaying car, she told me in a low, scolding voice how I had disobeyed and frightened her.

A slap across the face can become an indelible memory. Some years later when I was in eighth grade and had taken more lumps and was surviving, I sat in art class, drawing and painting what Sister Mary Ethelbert explained were "axial balances." She had us draw a vertical line, then a horizontal line near the bottom so it looked like an inverted cross. Then we made designs—ovals, circles, petals, whatever—and carefully balanced them on each side of the vertical line. Then we added more on the horizontal line until we had distributed our images in perfect symmetry and we had a design. I wasn't progressing well with mine. It was small and tentative and not much to look at. Sister Mary walked down the aisle, and when she saw my work, she slapped me hard across the face.

Why did those two slaps--Ma's at the concert and this nun's over a drawing—make a memorable dent? Corporal punishment was as common as rain in those days, as well as kids doing violence to each other. Why does my sister Anne still remember the nurse slapping her face when her leg was in traction?

I still see myself as unable to draw or paint. My angry mother seldom hit me but she showed me how to lash out when scared and confused, blaming someone, bullying people you love the most and who are trying to love you the most. That damaged me. It's a terrible example.

5

School

During the summer of 1940, Mary Lou walked me across the street to St. Mark Parish School and introduced me to Sister Mary Lawrence. My Catholic school education would be eight years of St. Mark and the Sisters of Notre Dame de Namur; four years of Christopher Columbus High and the Franciscan priests and brothers; and four years with the Jesuits at Boston College. While I would eventually study at Columbia and Harvard, it was the nuns, the Franciscan priests, and most of all the Jesuits who scrubbed me up and got me ready for life.

Sister wanted to see me that day to get me ready for her first grade a month or so later. Ma had held me out of kindergarten at the local public school. Other families might have been reluctant to mingle with the Protestant kids, but not my mother. More likely, she wanted her youngest and last to be home with her. So I needed a bit of remediation. Sister had me count to twenty several times, then we read a few words and she got me used to the intimidating look of the nuns in the long, black, ballooning robes they called habits—flowing black veils resting on head and shoulders, and the incongruous white fan-shaped, starched bibs that circled their upper body and hid any semblance of womanhood.

In first grade I learned that my clothes were odd. Most of them came in the parcel post in great boxes from Mrs. Sweetser. There would be small hunting jackets and golfing outfits and flashy tweeds—things that working-class kids didn't wear. There was a navy blue coat with gold buttons and red chevrons on the sleeve that matched one sent to my sister Anne. When we wore them, everyone smiled and called us the sailor twins. But at school some neighbor-hood kid said my coat was a girl's. (It did button wrong on the front, but how did he know?) I dreaded wearing those coats and jackets that came in the parcel post. But Ma said they were worn by the finest children in Boston, and who was I to turn them down?

—

My family lived for St. Mark Parish and the Catholic Church. Ma was a member of the altar society and the Sodality (as well as recording secretary of a Boston group of Cape Breton women called the Segher Charity Club). Dad was in the Knights of Columbus, the St. Vincent DePaul Society, and head usher at 7:30 a.m. Sunday Mass for thirty years up to the week he died. All six kids attended the parish school, and the three girls continued on with the Notre Dame nuns at Sts. Peter and Paul High School in South Boston. John was accepted at The Boston Latin School, a high school older than Harvard and the best in Boston to this day. Donald went to Dorchester High and dropped out in his junior year to join the navy before the war ended. I went to a high school taught by the Franciscans.

We saw the nuns every day except Saturday, were with them in the safe ha-vens of school and church. They were loving, devout women, but some could be intimidating, intolerant, rigid, and unforgiving. They used rulers or the back of a hand to correct you. The Franciscans at my high school sometimes added a swift kick with their sandaled foot. Some days you went through life with a sense of sin for doing—or not doing—something small. But school was a safe place where you knew the boundaries as far as the teachers were concerned. The students were another matter.

I was teased, bullied, and "de-pantsed" often as a kid. I was the youngest and smallest in my class and in my neighborhood gang, and that may have been enough to make me the target. Perhaps there was more. Ma babied me. Perhaps I didn't make the tormentors pay a heavy enough price to stop, or I wasn't sharp enough to see where a game was heading. There were lots of in-cidents. Because my winter woolen pants chafed me and caused a rash, I used to wear pajama bottoms that showed at the pants cuff. That must have made me fair game. I can't recall this in any detail, but it must have been one reason for the depantsing. The hazing wasn't a constant and it wasn't directed by any single kid, but it did go on for years.

I was in second grade, six and a half years old, when the war came.

On Sunday, December 7, 1941. I would have taken my weekly bath and, wrapped in a big towel, come down to the living room to sit in the sunlight on an upholstered stool in front of the Philco console. Sunday was when we listened to the weekly radio shows that filled our lives—preachers and comics, suspense shows and soap operas. This Sunday, the broadcast was different. I heard the clipped, staccato voices of newsmen and announcers who would become a part of daily life. I understood little of it, just that it was bad news.

It was not long before the single men who had been spending much of their time looking for jobs came through the neighborhood in military uniforms. Front windows displayed the blue and white nylon squares that signified the home of a serviceman, with one blue star for each member. Soon many showed gold stars meaning a son had been killed in action.

Dad, 49-years old with six young kids, became an air raid warden with a white helmet that said "CD" on it and a badge, number 4790. He had a billy club, a military flashlight, and a long pole that enabled him to extinguish the gas streetlamps during air raid drills. He patrolled the street, searching out leaks of light from the houses. We kept all the lights out and draped blankets across the windows, but Donald would go to an attic window and shine a flashlight on Dad as he walked past.

At school time was devoted to students telling tales of adventure and risk and deprivation, mostly for the benefit of the nuns, who were starved of particulars. V Mail from the front was heavily censored, arriving as a photocopy with a heavy black line through any mention of location or operation. Students told of their participation in the monthly paper drives, where trucks cruised through the neighborhoods and fathers supervised and kids scrambled about, tossing bundles of scrap newspaper onto the truck bed. They told how much they got for their enormous balls of saved tinfoil turned in at the Victory Center, or the price that a tin of fat drippings was bringing.

We had small paste-in books for collecting war savings stamps at ten cents each. When filled, the books could be converted to US savings bonds like the ones the movie stars and other celebrities urged us to buy. More precious were the ration stamps issued to each family to purchase meat, butter, sugar, coffee, and some canned foods. For those who had automobiles a windshield sticker showed if they were essential to the war effort, and gas ration stamps were issued.

I waited each week in hour-long lines outside Kennedy's, the dairy store in Codman Square, when a shipment of butter came in. The line was full of pushing housewives, and I soon learned to push along with the best of them and even to use humor when I felt the resentment toward an eight-year-old standing in for his mother. I remember once getting a laugh and a bit of recognition when I found myself surrounded and dwarfed by the taller women just as we got close to the counter. In a loud voice I said, "Would you please take your elbow out of my ear!" The counterman handed me a hand-cut slice of butter in waxed paper.

Between scrap drives and standing in rationing lines, there was plenty to do and new purpose to life. Everyone was working. Older girls took over men's jobs in offices, shops, and on assembly lines. High school girls and boys got part-time work at stores and offices. Dad was offered a higher-paying job as a carpenter at the Charlestown Navy Yard. His boss pleaded with him to stay, saying the war would soon be over, that he had a lifetime job with Summerfield's Furniture. He stayed. It sounds grim, but wasn't so bad for a kid. And the second summer of the war, in 1943, I had the best experience of my young life.

6

Patsy Hackett

In the spring of 1943 Ma got a letter from her benefactor and former employer, Mrs. Violet Shepley Sweetser of Brookline, asking if Ma would run the Sweetser family vacation home that summer, in Marion, Massachusetts, north of Cape Cod. She was to be housekeeper for two of the Sweetser daughters and a third young woman from Boston. They were now grown, the oldest daughter Julianna and her friend, Susan Story, with babies; Patsy alone. Their men were marine officers in the Pacific. It would be a nostalgic summer, far from war. Julianna had a three-year-old, so my sister Mary Lou, who would turn thirteen that August and was along as maid, sometimes helped as babysitter. I was invited when Ma said she couldn't leave me at home. So Dad worked all summer at Summerfield's and ran the house for two sons and two daughters between the ages of nine and fifteen, while Ma, Lou, and I lived the good life on the South Shore.

I remember the day we arrived at the big, gray, cedar-shingled house overlooking Buzzard's Bay. My mother worked in the kitchen surrounded by sunlight and knotty pine. She placed fresh broiler chickens in the stove and served them with bright green peas from the garden. This place was unlike anything I had experienced in my life.

There was Tara, the chestnut mare, and three different dogs that ranged the acres of the estate and came home to their mistresses. The ladies then tweezered ticks and bloodsuckers from their coats and dropped the parasites into a basin of water to thrash and drown. There was a lean man in overalls, Mr. Ellis, who had a farm at the end of our road where I took our garbage each morning and, under his supervision, fed it to piglets. I remember day sails in a sleek, skimming, boom-swinging boat. ("Ready about…Helm's alee!") I remember drives in the beach wagon or the pickup, and what seemed lavish shopping trips to Wareham. Because I brought a case of poison ivy with me from Dorchester, and it spread from head to toe, I spent the first weeks sitting on the private beach, unable to swim in the warm bay waters. I remember memorable dinners in the kitchen after Ma served the Sweetsers, the food fresh and sweet from the garden or from the truck farmer.

With Lou

I spent long days roving the manicured lawns down to the beach or the adjacent woods by the guest house that everyone called the playhouse. Sometimes I was on my own and sometimes with the gardeners who killed snakes with their rakes and held them up to impress me.

One evening Julianna, Patsy, and Sue Story planned an island party at sunset for the crowd from the yacht club, including some men home on leave. With great anticipation, the girls gathered every young friend they could find for what would be the reunion of the summer. Handsome kids, barely out of their teens, many with husbands overseas, seen only in the slim packets of scribbled V-mails from unknown places.

The crowd gathered, those who had played and lived and loved before war interrupted, now talking excitedly in this beautiful house, collecting the picnic baskets my mother had assembled, eager to head out for a late night on a nearby island. But before dusk the sky lowered and a storm threatened. Before the boats could launch, Ma entered the living room and announced to the guests that they should not go to the island in this weather.

"Roll up the rugs and have your picnic here, where it is safe," she said.

I heard the pleading voices:

"Oh Asha", the three said in unison, using the name they had given Ma as babies. "Please!"

"Asha, we'll be close by."

"Asha, this is our only chance this summer!"

My mother was quiet, unrelenting, budging not an inch. The island was not a good idea in this weather under these circumstances, she insisted. They could roll up the rug and turn on the Victrola.

This farm girl from Nova Scotia who hadn't finished high school, who had a passel of kids and an untutored husband to worry about—was just the hired help. She never flat out told them no, they could not go. If they had gone to the island and come home in one piece, she would not have told Mrs. Sweetser in all likelihood. But once she had given her guidance, the girls gave in.

Ma was happy, purposeful, all that summer. Was she quiet because one did not raise one's voice in the house of the wellborn? Or because there was no reason to yell? (She did yell at Lou out of upstairs earshot.) Was she cooking so well and caring for a house so well because it was her job, or because she was happy? She had just two of her own kids that summer, a handsome, well-furnished house to run, a generous budget, and the admiration and respect of those around her from the upper class. That helped if it did not cure her depression.

One of my fondest memories of that summer was of Patsy Hackett—athletic, self-assured, pretty and vain; her dark brown hair showing light streaks from the sun. She was a cover girl who endorsed Camel cigarettes in four-color back-page ads in *Life* or *Look* or *The Saturday Evening Post.* I have one such ad. There she was in full riding gear, jumping a horse, receiving a silver trophy. The ad copy read: "Experience is the best teacher—in jumping a horse or choosing a cigarette, says the super experienced Pat Hackett." In the colored photo her smiling face was bracketed by a riding crop in her left hand and a cigarette in her right hand, by her lips. A bubble of words floated above her head, in which she stated that the wartime shortages were a real experience, and of all the brands she'd smoked, Camels were the best. At the bottom of the page, next to the open Camel pack, the ad copy said "More doctors smoke Camels than any other cigarette."

Patsy took me to the stable and showed me Tara, brown and beautiful with a white star on her forehead and big, liquid, brown eyes that took me in. Tara nuzzled my shoulder and ate a piece of apple from my hand. Patsy showed me how to measure oats, put them in a bucket, and feed them to Tara, then to undo the rope across her stall and lead her to the pasture. I did it every day.

Patsy was newly married and not tied down with children. She spent the summer riding, sailing, playing tennis, and gallivanting. I remember one tense day when she went to the pasture to bridle Tara, who ran away, perhaps sensing her owner's mood. Patsy went after Tara, threw the bridle, and missed. She stood and called Tara. The horse came part way and shied. Patsy tried to lasso Tara with the bridle, but could not. I retreated to the house--where everyone was watching. It seemed to go on like this for an hour. Finally Patsy got Tara, saddled her, and took off at a ferocious pace. When she returned much later, Tara was soaked with sweat, her eyes fearful. Patsy stabled her and walked away without brushing or grooming or soothing the animal. I stayed away from the barn for the rest of the day.

—

Late on another morning, my mother sent me to the front of the house with a message for the ladies. When I found no one on the first floor, I climbed the stairs and headed for the sound of running water. As I passed a door, there was Patsy, standing full frontal as they say, looking at the shower—bare white skin below her tanned shoulders, startling, full breasts, and a blur of dark below. I turned and ran back to the kitchen, told my mother I couldn't find anyone, went to my room, and took a nap. Lou woke me after a while, smiling. She asked me about my visit upstairs. Patsy had told her, and laughed. I had forgotten about it after my nap. But Lou reminded me and said everyone was laughing about it. I went to the front of the house many times that summer, but never again above the first floor.

At Christmas Patsy sent me a present—a bone-handled hunting knife in a leather sheath, with a sharp, glittering six-inch blade—that Ma let me keep. I still had my teddy bear and would for more years. But Patsy's knife was part of a passage. I never saw Patsy again except on the back pages of magazines. I don't remember what happened to the knife, but I sure hope I wrote Patsy Hackett a thank-you note--for everything!

7

John and Donald

John left for the seminary as I entered fifth grade.

He had been a big part of my life, riding me places on the crossbar of his bike, teaching me some of the things he'd learned in Boy Scouts. He looked up "James" in a book, found it was rooted in the name Jacob, and started calling me Jake—the name I'm still called by many Dorchester folks. When my cat went missing I was inconsolable, and John took me to the Ringling Brothers, Barnum and Bailey Circus at the Boston Garden, my first time. We would go on short hikes with his buddies, me in the role of mascot. From my earliest memories, I see John and Mary Lou watching out for me, quietly caring for me. I don't remember a thing about his departure but he was always on my mind.

John wrote to me often. The summer I was in Marion he wrote this:

Dear Jim,

Your letter was swell. I'm glad your poison ivory (sic) is all better. You must be having a swell time. I was promoted at school, and now I'm working full time every day except Sunday at Mike's Market. Donald has his arm out of the cast now, and between Margie and Mike's, he is pretty busy. I will be going to camp pretty soon. Down at camp, I will be in charge of four cabins and thirty-two Boy Scouts. I ought to have a good time…

They had a famous flying fortress, the Memphis Belle at the East Boston airport. [It] has bombed the Nazis and the Japs all over the world. I betcha the horse is your friend because you give him his food. I am waiting for you to come home so you can tell me all about the raft and the boats and the animals and the beach and everything…

When he left home three years later, the letters continued, despite the pressure of studies and the cloister of seminary life. He wrote on plain notepaper and started each page by making a cross at the top. The return address was "St. Clement's Hall, Brighton." In December 1945, he wrote,

Dear Jim,

This is me. How are you? I hear you've been sick since I left home…I hope you're all better by now. I know you don't want to miss any school (Ha ha). How'd you like the big snowstorm? I'll bet that was a sudden ending for your football-playing. I suppose you're coasting down the street now.

And there would be a pep talk:

Mom was telling me you passed your Latin, and you're going to be an altar boy. Nice going. I'm glad you made it…It's a wonderful privilege…There aren't many people who can be so close to God in the tabernacle…You represent all the people in the Church at that Mass…picked from all those people to talk to God and help say the Mass for them…Only the priest gets more blessings than the altar boy…I know when you're serving you won't forget me in your prayers. I have to go now. I'm waiting on tables this week. If you have any free time, drop me a line.

Yours, John.

He was devout—"religious"—from early on. Perhaps that was his role as the surviving oldest after the loss of Donald Joseph Jr. John had his vocation in mind very early.

During dinners in our overheated, noisy kitchen with Ma nervously ferrying pots of food, dinnerware clanging loudly on the enameled zinc tabletop, kids complaining about their siblings as they worked off the day's frustrations; John would say, "Offer it up" and pause, then add, "you morons!" with a righteousness that made you feel responsible. He was quick to judge at times, the reaction of a teenager.

It was hard to follow in his wake. I joined Boy Scout Troop 41 at St. Mark, where John had been an Eagle Scout. Fred Blackden, the scoutmaster, "motivated" me with unfavorable comparisons to my oldest brother. On the first camp-out, he told me I was having trouble with a hike John would have aced. . He put his hand around my leg and asked if it was weak. I dropped out of Scouts; never got beyond Tenderfoot. Donald had gotten this treatment every day—at Scouts, at school, at church, and most devastating of all, from Ma at home. Donald was tall, athletic, and slim, but if he missed a step or moved slowly, she called him a lummox, which *Webster's* defines as "a clumsy, stupid person." John, on the other hand, was small and wiry, and each was in a different crowd of kids. But they were close enough that they worked jobs for each other.

Donald also separated from the competition. Instead of Boy Scouts, he excelled in the Junior Police Association, where a cop affectionately nicknamed him "Donald Duck," and to this day he is known in Dorchester as Ducky. John went to Boston Latin, the most elite school in the city, with a tough entrance exam and tough teachers who pushed students hard. Donald went to ordinary Dorchester High, skipped school often, and signed his own report cards. When a teacher came to our house one night to confront him in front of his parents, Ducky said, "Donald J. Doyle. That's my name!"

In grammar school, both John and Donald worked before and after school to help support the family. John led the way in giving the Doyle kids a good name and in making lifelong contacts. But Donald was the entrepreneur. He always had several jobs, several grown-ups who depended on his reliability.

Donald went to Barney Gack's news delivery agency at six o'clock weekday mornings, picked up his assigned bundle, and stood in front of Ogar's Drugs selling the *Globe, Post,* and *Herald* to the morning crowd. Then he walked across Dorchester Avenue to the Golden Ring Coffee Shop, unlocked the front door, started the coffee, and kneaded the raw doughnut dough. The owner, Roy, showed up with the crowds, and Ducky headed up the street to St. Mark's School, smelling of dough.

John had started working at Roy's first, then Donald added a Whiting's Milk route to his jobs. If Mike the milkman was hung over and late, Donald went to the barn, hitched the horse to the wagon, and started the route. The horse knew every house stop, and Donald knew what to deliver. Mike showed up to relieve Donald for school, unless it was snowing hard. When there was no school, Ducky often did the entire route, also on weekends. After school he hung around Barney Gack's store watching Roy, Barney, Mike, and the other merchants play cards, which led him to more paying jobs. He stopped by the merchants on Dorchester Avenue to ask if they needed a delivery boy or a helper. Mike Connolly, of Connolly's Market, sent word to my mother that he had a job for the boy who had inquired. She sent John. "The kid was a lot bigger than you," Mike said. He hired John and soon Donald as well, and they became the dependable delivery team from Connolly's Market.

Once John left for the seminary in 1945, I saw less and less of him and of Donald, who that year quit Dorchester High and joined the navy. He was seventeen, and the war was still on, although it ended before he finished boot camp. When they were both home on leave, they sat on a bed in the attic bedroom and played cribbage together for hours on end. *Fifteen two, fifteen four, fifteen six.* I never learned the game. I didn't much like it.

8

Heebing

In 1947, a returning veteran bought the house at 41 Samoset Street from our neighbors the Nesdales, and under rent control rules, he could move us out to occupy. By that point, the house had rats in the cellar and cockroaches in the kitchen. Dad put down big traps in the dark cellar and green roach powder in cracks around the flat. The new landlord evicted us.

Summerfield's, caught in the postwar inflation and the popularity of cheaper, assembly-line furniture, closed the mill room that Dad ran, no longer in need of the tall cutting and shaping machines, the rotary blades whirring and my father supervising the carpenters who could replace any furniture part or make whole pieces. He was laid off, ironic since friends had shown him that by moving to the shipyards, he could make more money and get more benefits. His bosses at Summerfield's had convinced him that those shipyard jobs would end with the war and that he had a lifetime job where he was. So he'd stayed put. Of course the shipyard jobs didn't end at all. The government wasn't going to lay off all those workers who had helped win the war.

Instead we got inflation. Some food prices doubled when controls were lifted, and there was a black market for those who had swag saved during the war and now wanted beef steaks and a new car. The housing crisis got worse. Strikes broke out in coal mines, on the railroads, and in the steel mills. Industries tried to keep wage controls even though price controls had buckled under market pressure.

A lot of what I'm telling here is based on dim memories and talks with my brothers and sisters. One memory is my own and still breaks my heart: a day with Dad walking the streets of downtown Boston in the factory district around the South End as he looked for a job. He was a fifty-five-year-old man who had always worked —before and during the Great Depression and the war that followed. He was the supervisor at Summerfield's for twenty years. We had pictures of him at the company picnics, in suit and tie, John and Donald in tow, sitting among his men. At times, he worked until he dropped. (Ducky tells how Dad was once taken to the hospital because of stomach pain that turned out to be gallstones. The doctors asked, "When did you have your heart attack?" (apparently one of his exhaustion illnesses, undiagnosed.)

Dad and I walked slowly, a heavy wooden toolbox on his shoulder. I would sit on a chair while he went to the office showing the boss his tools, opening the box he'd made out of ash with a mahogany veneer, an ornate brass lock, his initials, *DJD,* engraved above. With John in the seminary and Donald in the navy, Lou working as a dental assistant, Cappy and Anne at St. Peter and Paul's High School in South Boston, and me still at St. Mark School, Joe Doyle was on the street. He found a job on an assembly line making cheap chairs and tables while he searched for something better.

—

It seemed that everyone was pissed off then. A lot of newly returned veterans were hanging around, members of the 52–20 club getting weekly bonus checks of $20 the first year after discharge. Many went back to school on the GI Bill, often living in steel Quonset huts on the edge of campus with their wives and babies. But the neighborhood taverns were also filled with vets every day. During the war, you could get a pack of Marvel cigarettes, or Wings, for ten cents, and we'd go into the woods by the train tunnel and smoke. By 1947, when we were twelve and thirteen, some of the boys were carrying packs of Lucky Strike. But we couldn't smoke in front of Crawford's—it was too public.

My gang had a football team and wore green and gold jerseys with *Apaches* lettered on the back. I didn't make the team and didn't have an Apache jersey. We used to stand in front of Crawford's Drug Store in the evening after supper. We would go in and have a five-cent raspberry Coke at the counter, then hang around outside and spit a lot. The twelve- and thirteen-year-old St. Mark's girls, who occupied the other wing of the school, had dark blue wool jackets that said *Mohicans* in white script on the back. They hung out on the street corner across from Crawford's. We pretended not to notice them. They did the same with us.

If you asked our parents, most would have said we were good kids, that we minded most of the time, did the chores, stayed out of trouble, and respected the nuns and the priests. For adolescents growing up in a working-class neighborhood in postwar Boston, we were innocents compared to many city kids.

So why did we do what we called heebing? I don't know who came up with the idea that spring evening, but I'm sure I said yeah with the same enthusiasm as the others. I don't know how we got on the subject of the Jews. We didn't know any, but that didn't stop us from echoing the anti-Semitism that was all around us at home, church, and school.

Someone said, "We should get a camel and put a sign on it that says 'Guns for the Arabs,' and we should ride it down Blue Hill Avenue." There was a lot of hooting at that idea.

Blue Hill Avenue was in Mattapan, a Jewish enclave, just as Fields Corner was an Irish one. People like the famous journalist Theodore H. White (*The Making of the President* series) and Nat Hentoff, the writer, grew up there. Both have written about the savage anti-Semitism that existed in the surrounding neighborhoods. The truth is that we didn't know a thing about Mattapan, except sometimes older kids walking home from Dorchester High came through there, and ladies would poke their heads out windows and ask the boys if they would come in and light the gas stove and would then pay them ten cents. It was because of the Jewish holidays, we were told. Nothing wrong with the stoves, you just had to be a gentile to light the stove on these days. The people were just as poor as us and just as worried about the housing shortage and jobs for the veterans and the A-bomb. Nobody in either neighborhood had much opportunity, but they had aspirations for their kids and hopes that times were going to get better now.

So one of us said, "Let's go heebing!"

Was I the only one who didn't know what that meant? We set off along the main avenues of Dorchester, a pack of adolescent lemmings spitting and cursing our way toward Mattapan. Someone produced a pack of Luckies and passed them around. We stopped, and someone produced a Zippo and we held the ceremony—lighting up two Luckies and passing them around, complaining that one or another of us had "put a lipper" on the cigarette, wetting the end. As the smallest and youngest kid, I struggled to keep up with these fellows, always hoping to be accepted.

Only later would I put some things together—the times before the war when they were selling Father Charles Coughlin's magazine *Social Justice* at every Catholic church, and how on Sundays our parents gathered around the radio and listened to his mesmerizing voice, his clarity, his answers to all problems. He began to rail against President Roosevelt and to defend Hitler, then he lost stature and his radio voice was silenced. But on those Sundays, as he unraveled mysteries about the world conspiracy and the secret protocols of the Jews, he would name the members of Stalin's politburo, and after every name he would say, "a Jew!" Jews, he said, were why we were poor and why there was a depression.

That evening we were clustered in front of the Mattapan Bowl-a-Drome when two Jewish boys walked out. I don't remember much about them except both were taller than me and they seemed neater; better dressed than us. They didn't say anything. They knew what was about to happen. There were six or more of us, and we surged forward. Someone swung a fist, and there was a skirmish. The Jewish kids either held their ground or perhaps were unable to retreat.

We broke it off quickly and headed out at a run for the grounds of the Cedar Grove Cemetery down the street. Once over the cast-iron pickets, we dispersed among the graves and the tree-lined paths. A police siren sounded and then stopped. The police didn't take these calls very seriously. We regrouped, headed across the cemetery to the trolley tracks, and there split up, each climbing down at a different overpass and mingling with the street traffic. I felt scared, soiled.

This was heebing.

Twenty years before, another kid was on the Mattapan streets, his family dirt poor, scratching to survive. His family picnicked in Franklin Park, too. But when he walked to the Codman Square Library-- like the Doyles would do later-- the Irish kids beat him up. He was a Jewish kid who lived on Erie Street and, he wrote many years later in one of his books, "Pure hellishness divided us" from the neighboring Irish kids. His name was Teddy White. He persisted and soon some Irish kids gave him safe passage to the library. Like my brother John after him, Teddy White went to The Boston Latin School, won a newsboy scholarship to Harvard from the Burroughs Foundation, graduated summa cum laude, became a war correspondent in China during World War II and one of the great journalists of his time.

In the 60s I met him on presidential campaigns. I learned from him and we became friends. He knew I was from Boston, but I never told him I was with the next generation of Irish kids beating up Jewish kids from Mattapan.

9

Damian

In the middle of that winter of 1947 we found a duplex apartment at 28 Pierce Avenue in nearby St. Anne's Parish. We moved in during a coal-miners' strike, and coal prices had skyrocketed. Dad hung a heavy blanket across the kitchen door opening, and we lived mostly in the kitchen, heated by a cooking stove, until we could afford delivery of coal.

In the first year there, Mary Lou left for the Sisters of Notre Dame novitiate in Waltham. I was in the back yard that day and during the picture-taking I started feeling sick. We left for Waltham with me riding with Lou in Eunice O'connor's car. Eunice was Lou's best friend and I guess we both knew that Lou would be gone for good. After we left the novitiate I lay in the back seat of the car and threw up all the way home.

So there were three kids in the flat at 28 Pierce Avenue. Cappy and Anne took a bus and then the subway to high school in South Boston. I walked an extra mile or so to St. Mark for my last year of grammar school. I hung out with classmates from Florida Street, near to me.

Before we moved, some kid had gotten me to join the Immaculate Conception Men and Boys Choir at the Jesuit church in downtown Boston. I was a good enough soprano to be accepted in a group of talented musicians. We practiced—hard—for two hours every Friday evening and another hour or two on Sunday before performing at the eleven-thirty High Mass. We practiced continually before major recitals—Theodore Dubois's cantata, *Seven Last Words of Christ*, on Good Friday, various *Alleluia* chorals at Easter, Christmas Solemn High Mass liturgies. We ate meals at the refectory and hung out in the dark, silent halls and rooms of the uncloistered part of the Jesuit residence, where the priests who taught at Boston College High School lived. With a few of the other boys I would visit nursing homes and do recitals for the old people. The choir had an eminent master named Ralph Jesco and a vigorous chaplain named Father Gildea. If I had stayed with it, Father Gildea would have gotten me a scholarship to Boston College High School, where the Jesuits would have worked my tail off, taught me how to study, and motivated me. But I stopped going to choir and went to movies on Friday nights, using the choir carfare money, hanging out with my Florida Street friends. I would bicycle to the Supreme Market for Ma, buy two cans of tuna fish and shoplift a third can and keep the change. I would also shoplift bags of candy—Good 'N Plenty, Tootsie Rolls, Nonpareils—and if it was Lent, when I was fasting from candy, I would put them in a box under my bed and save them until noon on Holy Saturday.

I was a stranger in St. Anne's Parish and my new neighborhood. A bike ride away was a shopping area where I encountered some older kids, a new group of bullies, who could be unaccountable at the shopping center, with no family connections and no one to watch what went on,. My bike was more important to me now, to travel the distance to St. Mark's and on solo rides or errands. The bullies stole it.

Dad had built that bike from parts. You couldn't miss it with its different colored frame and chrome fenders, a mangled wire basket from a collision. I had no lock for it and when it disappeared, I went looking, found it with two of the bullies and demanded it back. They were four or five years older than me, strapping kids, and they pushed me around, said it was their bike and to never come near them again. If I had known how to do it, I could have found a friendly cop or a priest or a bigger kid and asked for help. Most likely these kids were known as trouble-makers. But I couldn't very well ask my overwhelmed Dad to help me, and I didn't know anyone else. I saw those kids and my bike around the shopping area all the time and it hurt—the brazen theft, the sense of my being alone and vulnerable on these new streets. I didn't get the bike back, but I can see that bike today.

—

A Fine Photography Studio was among the shops a few blocks down the hill from Pierce Avenue, across from the five-and-ten-cent store. The proprietor was a small and slender man who wore bifocals in gold frames. He was perhaps in his forties, soft-spoken, a native of New Brunswick. I'll call him Damian. As I walked by one day he asked if I would hold the squeegee he was using while he sponged down the glass on his front display window. He thanked me and said to come by the next day, he was going to test some new film and would take some portraits of me. So I did, and he put me in a stiff-backed swivel chair like secretaries use, turned on the big studio lights, and got behind his Graflex portrait camera. The next day he gave me the pictures, showing a round, freckle-faced kid with outsized ears and a half smile, a dress shirt open at the collar, a rip on the left shoulder. I started hanging around the photo studio after that.

. Damian gave me an old folding Kodak and a roll of film and we would develop my pictures. He taught me about composition and darkroom techniques, how to use an enlarger, how to "burn in" details such as clouds or underexposed parts. I began reading his photography magazines. With his encouragement I submitted pictures to the monthly photo contest of *Camera Cubs and Camera Teens* magazine and for a picture of a wharf I won first prize, an Ansco Fed-Flash camera outfit,. I still have a picture Damian helped me print on fine 5 by 7 photo paper—a steam train departing Neponset Station taken from a bridge above, the white plume of steam and the gleaming tracks perfectly framing the big, black locomotive.

After a deep snow, I took pictures of the finest houses off Adams Street, blanketed in white. Damian gave me a negative template that said, *"Season's Greetings from Our House to Your House,"* and we framed the house negatives in the template and printed them. In his darkroom I made a dozen greeting-card prints of each house, then took them to the owners and asked a dollar for a dozen. Everyone bought. (I should have asked $1.50.)

Damian was now my mentor. I used the proceeds from the Christmas pictures to go into Boston to a store on Bromfield Street frequented by professional photographers. There I bought Damian a pair of magnifying glasses to replace the monocle loupe he was using. He was genuinely touched.

I could hang around the studio anytime I wanted. I learned a great deal from him, and I was safe from the streets and the bullies. But one day during a quiet time in the darkroom, Damian started the tickling game which led to the excitement of being captured, then his hands unzipping my pants and gently taking control of my privates. I didn't resist. Afterward, everything went back to normal, and we made photographic prints, his hands cupped under the enlarger's lens manipulating the beam, changing the image on the paper into more shades of grays, different textures of light and dark.

He had seduced me, and he was to continue playing the tickling game on occasion but not each time I came by. I knew what was happening but not what it meant. I don't recall feeling any change in our relationship. His gentle predations, his betrayal, was limited and careful. I did not resist and he was careful not to press on to further abuses. Soon I was preoccupied with high school and new friends, and then we moved back to St. Mark Parish once Dad got a steady job. I didn't say good-bye to Damian. I just didn't go back to Fine Photography and its darkroom.

—

The kids in my St. Mark class who lived around Florida Street, on the edge of the parish, became my gang. I was the smallest and the youngest, but these kids accepted me as an equal, listened to my ideas, and started protecting me when we got in trouble. None of us talked about our families much, but I figured out that these kids had a lot less home life than I did—violent dads or parents who drank, other unstated troubles. These kids were reluctant to head home at the end of the day, and they had a hunger for adventures that consisted of petty lawbreaking and giving the finger to authority.

This was the beginning of my new life of hopping trucks and trolley cars, more shoplifting, fleeing from the cops and lying about where I was going or where I had been. Ma and Dad were busy trying to hold things together. When Father Gildea called my mother to tell her how disappointed he was that I was no longer coming to choir, I told her my voice was changing and I was embarrassed, unable to perform. About this time I decided Ma wasn't counting the change after errands and I started keeping some. Then I started going into her pocketbook and taking change. Twenty five or fifty cents was a good allowance in those days. I helped myself.

The electric streetcars along Neponset Avenue had stationary running boards and accommodating rear steps where it was easy to perch. My new friends taught me how to step aboard as the car slowed, keep my head down, ride to my destination, and step off when it stopped. If it didn't stop when you wanted off, you could yank the trolley pole until the grooved wheel at the top slipped off the overhead power line and stopped the car. Then you disappeared before the motorman emerged to put the trolley line right.

We would also hop aboard the heavy, open-back delivery trucks when they stopped at a traffic light. We'd boost each other up and ride with the cargo for miles, north to Boston or south to Quincy, then hop another truck home or to an El station. We walked in the streetcar tunnels in the city, where the dangers were a train coming when there was no niche to stand in, or a transit cop catching you.

Once a plainclothes cop was standing there when the streetcar stopped, and I was the only kid who didn't run. He grabbed me off the back of the trolley and pulled me to the sidewalk, demanding my name and address. He searched me and found a green leather wallet that Lou had given me—a girl's wallet. That convinced him I had stolen it. I stood there terrified and fumbling my answers until Red Hastings, our leader and the first one away from the scene, came sauntering back.

"Hi, Jake," he said. "What's the trouble?" He was polite and brimming with confidence. He assured the officer that he would take me home and see that this didn't happen again. And I was let go, in Red's custody.

I would always be the last aboard the truck or trolley, and one or more of the other kids would help me up. There were some close scrapes. Bumpsy Gallagher couldn't get aboard a truck one time, and his feet were dragging on the ground. Red Hastings went to the rear window of the cab and started knocking and yelling for the driver to stop, but the driver and his partner just laughed, thinking, I suppose, we just wanted off at a convenient place. For a few miles Bumpsy struggled, crying, raising his legs until exhausted, then dragging his feet until the pain forced him to raise his legs again. Finally he fell into the roadway, shaken and bruised but able to get up and walk away. There must have been times when I came close to injury or even early death. "Close calls," they are labeled, and most of us remember times on the highway or on the water when, even as adults, we came a little closer to harm than we would like.

It was about this time that Dad, always devout, started following the rules of the Third Order of St. Francis. He never spoke of it, but he wore a scapular, two brown cloth medals on a slender cord draped around the neck and worn next to the skin, to symbolize the brown garment worn by monks. St. Francis of Assisi (1181–1226) was one of the most powerful and charismatic figures in Catholicism. He stood for social justice, assisting the poor and peacemaking, and his legacy continues today. I have no idea how Dad came to the Third

Order practice, but it is designed to allow civilians—lay people in the church with family obligations—to live fuller spiritual lives. Perhaps Dad went to a retreat at St. Mark preached by a Franciscan father, or maybe he learned about it through the St. Vincent DePaul Society that collected food and clothing and quietly gave them to the poorest and neediest and most troubled families in St. Mark parish. (These would have included some of my classmates and buddies, although I was never aware of it.) Dad learned and recited daily some liturgical prayers, which meant that he was quietly becoming literate.

So I was an adolescent surrounded by the Catholic religion; not mature enough to reflect on it and too young and pissed off to follow the example. But something—luck, karma, grace, the constant prayers of family—rescued me.

After Lou had graduated from St. Peter and Paul's High School in South Boston, she trained as a dental technician. Cappy worked for the phone company saving money to pay for nursing school, then trained at Boston City. Anne was in her senior year, with that long commute to Southie. If my brothers had been home, they would have been working and contributing, and John would have been keeping an eye on me. But they were gone, and I was floundering. I did deliver newspapers, but it wasn't a serious job like Donald and John had at my age. It was *The Dorchester Argus*, a weekly that went to every home. I'd go around and try to collect and a small number of people would give me the dime. I would turn in the money and get some of it back, but not very much.

Once when he was home on vacation, John came into my room and asked me to read an article from the *Saturday Evening Post* and then immediately left for his daily visit to St. Anne's Church to pray. The article was addressed to parents and told them how to explain the facts of life to their children. I read it, but when John returned from church, he didn't mention it.

Before she left for the convent, Mary Lou went to work for a dentist, and once she gained his confidence, she told him about me and my teeth. I hadn't been to a dentist since I was five because on my first visit to the free dental clinic at the Codman Square Library, the student from Tufts Dental had deeply frightened me without even knowing it. I was scared, and he was talking to another student working at the next chair, when he put pliers in my mouth, grabbed a tooth, yanked it, and then threw it across the room where it clanked against a waste bin. I don't remember it hurting, but I was frightened by the experience.

The nuns at St. Mark had a system for getting kids dental care. Once a year, a friendly parish dentist, Dr. Dempsey, came to class and examined teeth. Instead of sterilized tongue depressers the nun gave him a supply of unsharpened pencils. He would take a fresh one, use it to look inside a mouth, tell the nun what he found and give the student that pencil. When we went home that day, the nun handed out permission slips to be signed by a parent allowing the child to go to a free dental clinic set up in the basement of the Codman Square library. I never took the slip home, so I never got on any list to go back to a dentist. By high school, my teeth were filled with rot. Now, Lou took me to her dental office and held my hand while her boss worked on tooth after tooth, week after week. That is a big reason why, on the day Lou left to enter the convent, I was sick to my stomach.

10

I was in high school when we moved back to St. Mark, to the first floor of a well-kept three-decker near Ashmont Station in the nicest neighborhood yet. The owners were down-easters who my parents knew, and the turmoil of our recent years seemed to be over.

Dorchester three-deckers were an architectural invention—apartments transformed into a house with porches front and back. The second and third floor front porches were called piazzas, and were often decorated with fancy wooden railings. A big step up. But…

—

Drink was a common enough medicine in Dorchester, and it turned out that this landlord was a serious alcoholic who went on binges. In good weather he would sit on the third-floor piazza with his drinking buddies, loud and boisterous. No problem for us, since we had always given our neighbors a wide berth. As a drinking bout would go on, his wife sought more than sympathetic listeners. The crisis came, and the landlord's wife enlisted Dad's help along with the police to intervene. Dad helped carry the man in a chair down the three flights and into an ambulance, where he was transported to Washingtonian Hospital, one of the first and best places in the country for treating addictions. When the landlord finally returned home, he seemed to be cured. But it wasn't long before the eviction notice came. He could not bear to have us in his house, a reminder of his shame. So no good deed goes unpunished. It's ironic, because Dad was not quick to judge others or theirs faults. And though he was not much of a drinker, he enjoyed a taste.

—

Once (before all this) Dad came home from a union meeting relaxed and happy. Ma was at Sodality. "Come on," he said, "sit with me while I eat dinner." He was funny, going on about this and that and not at all his sober self. I realized he was tipsy—there must have been beer at the meeting—and after listening uncomfortably and humoring him, I broke down and cried, tears streaming down my face.. "Aw, don't cry," he said. He was sad for me, for not being able to enjoy his mood. And I am sad when I think of it.

Once again we were refugees coping as supplicants while Dad searched for a stable home. He soon found 12 Penhallow Street, the second and third floor of a duplex in one of the best sections of Dorchester, by Melville Avenue.

I resumed my delinquent phase, still palling around with the wildest element of the Dorchester Apaches, my classmates from St. Mark. We had graduated and gone on to different schools, but the same corner was still our turf; the Mohicans were still our consorts; the parish dances were a big part of every weekend. Drinking was forbidden at social occasions, but a growing part of life for some. So it came to pass that on Good Friday night, I invited Bumpsy, Red Hastings, and a few others to my house for drinks. My parents would be safely ensconced in church for the lengthy Good Friday liturgy. I thought this was a great idea.

At my party that fateful Good Friday evening, I passed around my parents' Four Roses rye, and we all partook of what in retrospect could be considered a sacrilegious ceremony. When we started to feel the buzz, and the excitement of this bold home invasion began to wear on us, we headed out to a nearby liquor store where homeless men loitered to serve underage hoods. We gave them the money, including their fee; then they went inside and purchased quarts of lager and presented us with the bags. We headed for the top of the nearby rapid transit tunnel, built above ground to avoid excavation costs, and fenced off, unreachable by car including police cruisers, a secluded place to loiter. Soon we could hear constant police sirens and knew cops were sweeping the area. We decided to split up.

As the youngest, the smallest, and the most inebriated, I made my usual boneheaded decision to walk alone down Melbourne Street, supposedly minding my own business, perhaps heading home--and undoubtedly weaving like the drunk that I was. A patrol car stopped and one of the cops threw me roughly in the back. They began questioning me about the break-in I had just perpetrated with my gang. By the time they got me to the Fields Corner Precinct, they had decided I was the perpetrator because I was drunk and despite my denials and groggy bewilderment--I hadn't broken into any store, nor had I done anything else criminal. They found my wallet—the ladies' green one Lou had given me and that I still carried. One of the officers slapped me across the face while the other one called the house (we now had a phone). He picked up my father and drove him to the precinct. Whether it was because of my Dad's earnest behavior and shame, my own confused, transparent inability to take part in any successful criminal enterprise, the lack of evidence against me, or perhaps the apprehension of other kids red-handed, I'll never know. But they put me in the back of the cruiser with Dad and drove us home. And what has stayed with me for a half century since is the picture of my father— the best role model a kid could have—sitting beside me dazed, broken, and saying in a soft voice, "Father, forgive them for they know not what they do."

Not long after, I went to a meeting of the Junior Holy Name Society, and with several others, signed "the pledge." Father Dunphy, a World War II chaplain and a pal, explained that we were promising not to use alcohol again before our twenty-first birthdays. For me, that was six years away, but I signed. I still hung out, but lots of the Apaches had taken the pledge, and we recognized the seamy side of buying bottles from alcoholic men, of hiding and drinking to no purpose.

Ma's upsets, her anger, migraines and lashing out, got better as her burdens lessened. Cappy and Anne were looking out for me. I had been extremely bratty toward Ann when we were younger. I'd pick a fight with her, and Ma would land on her. She remembers exactly when the taunting stopped. I was bragging about being one of the boys who, at Malibu Beach, would throw girls in the water. She sat me down and told me never to throw a girl into the water—especially if she was not wearing a bathing suit like her friends—because girls ' bodies were different. She says I was wide-eyed, that I understood, and started treating her with more respect.

Anne became the family member treating me special. Birthdays weren't celebrated in our house, but when I turned fifteen, Anne was eighteen and dating a rich kid. She got him to host a birthday party for me at his impressive home, and I've never forgotten it. Seven years later, when I headed off to Naval Officer Candidate School, Anne contacted all my friends from Boston College—no easy task—and threw a surprise party at her home and it was an unforgettable occasion. Four years later when I headed to New York for graduate school, I failed to find a buyer for my 1958 Hillman Minx convertible. I urgently needed the $1,000 I might get for it to pay my tuition, so Anne parked it safely in her garage, found a buyer, and sent me the proceeds.

11

Christopher Columbus

Christopher Columbus High School was across the city in the heart of old Boston. Starting in the fall of 1948, the El trains that had taken me to the beach and to choir practice now took me each weekday to Haymarket Square, the central market. I walked through the North End, the Italian quarter, one square mile with 40,000 people wedged in the apartment buildings along narrow streets crowded with delivery trucks and littered with cardboard box parts and the occasional spoiled grapefruit, broccoli stem, or squashed carrot; avoiding foraging cats, dog poop, and the litter from rows of markets and commercial shops.

The limp, pink bodies of skinned lambs and rabbits hung from hooks in front of the butcher shops. The bakeries smelled of fresh bread, rows of exotic cakes and cookies glistened in pastry shop windows. Beneath their awnings, produce stores were lined with bins of grapes, oranges, dates, fennel, celery, cauliflower. Fish stores stacked fresh cod, halibut, swordfish, and shrimp on beds of ice. There were cigar stores and newsstands, and Italian lunch rooms offering things called gelato and spumoni.

Above these shops were the old tenements whose bricks were gray from soot, three or four stories high with tiny balconies, laundry flapping in the breeze. It was a big, sprawling, tight neighborhood. People knew each other, and non-Italians were strangers. The benches in the small parks and the paved playgrounds were dotted with old men talking, smoking, observing, and playing bocce on the worn earth. Mothers leaned out windows to call their kids home. (Fifty years later the North End was cleaned up and well off with a fifth of the population, but the culture endured. A televised pasta ad celebrated it with a mother leaning out of her apartment window calling her son home for dinner yelling "Anthonyyyyy!" It reminded me of Charley Donovan, a class-mate who when we would be walking from Haymarket to Christy he would mock the surroundings by cupping his hand around his mouth and shouting "Hey, Rocco!")

Christopher Columbus, or "Christy", as we called it, was in the middle of this on Tileston Street. It was a three-story brick fortress that had seen its best days. Half was a central Catholic high with boys from parochial schools across the city, as many Irish from Dorchester as Italian from the neighborhood. The other half was a high school taught by nuns for the neighborhood girls. The girls were taught by nuns and the boys by Franciscan priests and brothers from a semi-nary in Lowell. They came from working families to teach the sons of working families. Other branches of the order are known for distinguished scholars, but these men seemed to have none of those ambitions nor the intellectual rigor of teaching orders like the Jesuits, the Christian Brothers who ran elite high schools in other cities, or the Holy Cross Fathers who were making Notre Dame into a first-rank college. Franciscans wear brown, floor-length robes tied at the waist with a white cord, and sandals (with socks in the winter)—the clothing of the Assisi poor. I don't know how I chose the school—most likely with the guidance of the Notre Dame nuns at St. Mark. The tuition was $25 a year, and that must have seemed affordable, but it never challenged me. I quickly tracked into the lower rung of students, didn't study much or learn how to do so.

The classrooms were old. There was no gym, no cafeteria. With the 45 minute subway commute, my days were long, with an element of boot camp. Minor corporal punishment was the standard, and some of the teachers liked to boot kids in the butt with their sandaled foot. In Latin class with Father John and biology class with Father Anthony, I spent a good deal of time kneel-ing in the front of the classroom because I had been talking, wisecracking, passing notes, or just making a point of not paying attention.

I learned a bit of science from a chemistry teacher named Father Emil who had a sense of humor, and some Dickens (*A Tale of Two Cities*) from an English teacher who spent much of the class rubbing his forehead and grimacing as if in pain. I remember the mindless (to me) memorization in Latin and French classes and the seeming inability of most teachers to get any of us excited about the material.

A common punishment was detention, which meant we traveled home on the subway in the winter dark during rush hour with the exhausted workers. Another was to write five hundred words on why one didn't do the homework or got caught doing something wrong. I remember an assembly at St. Leonard's, the church next door. We filed in, talking loudly, laughing, slightly out of control. The principal, Father Thomas, stood in the pulpit and watched the scene for a good five minutes, and when things started to quiet down, he announced that all would have to write a thousand-word, six-page theme on proper conduct in church.

Knowing the themes would be tossed in the rubbish without a glance, I wrote a fresh sentence at the top and bottom of each page, and then filled in the pages with gibberish such as "When I call my cat I say, 'here, kitty, kitty'" over and over. Then, like the arrogant dope that I was, I exhibited the finished product to my classmates, who thought it so funny that some of them shared it with one of the Franciscans.

Father Thomas suspended me; told me to go home and have my mother call him. It was springtime, and I stopped on the way home at Savin Hill Station, walked to Malibu Beach, and sat in the sun for a while. Then I went home and told Ma she had to call the school. I watched her as apparently she heard the damning details from Father Thomas. She hung up. She looked at me. And then she laughed out loud.

I wasn't studying or doing homework, but I was getting into, and away with, a lot of trouble. At the kitchen table I would counterfeit the brown "car checks" which students used to ride the subway. At the turnstiles, there was a box to toss in your car checks as you passed. A sheet of 20 cost $1.00. I pocketed the dollar and fashioned them out of grocery bags marked with broad pencil strokes to look like printing, then cut to size. The MTA changed the color to green, so I procured green paper and continued my counterfeiting.

After school I hung out with my St. Mark buddies—the delinquent crowd I fell in with when I quit the Immaculate Conception Men and Boys Choir. A fellow choir member and neighbor, Paul Gavin, kept telling me I could have parlayed my Jesuit connections into a scholarship to Boston College High School, which was closer to home, a first-rate school, and a ticket to college. This made no impression. The principal at Christy would come into our class and say, "Those of you planning to go to college, raise your hand." Then he would glower at me and say, "Doyle! Raise your hand!"

———

I found an after-school job as a stock boy in a wallpaper warehouse in the North End, a distributor who supplied retail stores. I stocked bins, counted out rolls to fill orders, cleaned the aisles, and ran errands. I learned the stock numbers of every style and color, and what styles particular stores wanted. The workforce consisted of Murray, the sleek, glossy manager, always in a shirt and tie despite the blue-collar surroundings; his plain-looking and plain-dressing wife Esther, daughter of the owner, who argued with her husband over the way he was running things; and me from three o'clock to five thirty each afternoon. It was lonely and intimidating because Murray and Esther were always uptight, alert to the possibility of mistakes or me "loafing," working too slow.

Once a week it was my job to take the Pitney-Bowes mail meter and a check to the post office down by North Station where a clerk would reset the meter. It was my only time away from the stock bins, and I tried to make the most of it. I perused every storefront—plumbing supplies, hardware supplies, used clothing stores, a welding shop, and the background hum of truck engines and brake screeches. Of course, Murray—or more likely Esther—was timing me. I returned with the postage meter one day, and Murray announced that he had happened to be on the street, and he had observed me dawdling. I was shocked and embarrassed, as if I'd been caught with my hand in the till. (There was no till. Their business was all credit.) Still, Murray liked me, and he told me there was a full time job waiting for me when I graduated, and that someday I would make $130 a week. Dad was making less than that.

The post-war world was beginning to change the country, to open up opportunities for the veterans who had the G.I. Bill and were using it to get a good education and a better life. But I hadn't gotten the memo about the possibilities. I was going through the motions in high school, mired in Cs and Ds and going nowhere.

Except for John, nobody was paying much attention to my lack of ambition. One day he telephoned me from the seminary to tell me he had arranged a job interview for me and how much I could learn at the State House and the people I would meet. I went to see St. Mark parishioner Paul Ryan, the owner of the State House News Service, who like everyone else, thought the world of my brother John. He hired me to be the after-school office boy (as John and then Donald had been). My world was transformed from drudgery to excitement, from aimlessness to an immediate understanding of what work could be and what education was about. Unless you have been a newspaperman, you don't know what a joy it can be.

The State House News Service and Paul Ryan are unique in my experience. Ryan was the first newsman I met who knew how to make money. He ran a news agency that consisted of himself, two full-time staff reporters, and others available on short notice to cover the state legislature—the Great and General Court of Massachusetts—for reporters from papers and broadcast stations. Whenever the House or Senate was in session, a News Service reporter sat near the presiding officer, pounding away on a "silent" typewriter—one whose keys had been cushioned to lessen the clack. He produced a running account of the debate, every ruling, and every vote. Wearing a shirt and tie and pressed pants, I would walk toward the podium, moving as unnoticed as a department store floorwalker, on the floor of the House and the Senate chambers I would gather up each page or "take," and hurry it upstairs to the SHNS office next to the press room. There I mimeographed copies and quickly distributed them into the slots in a huge cabinet labeled with the names of most of the daily and some weekly papers in the state. I got to work at three o'clock, just as evening deadlines were approaching. The state house reporters from Boston, Worcester, Springfield, and Pittsfield; the wire service reporters from the Associated Press and United Press; the political reporters from the radio stations—all would be waiting by the cabinet to snatch the take from me before I could slip it into their slot. Then I would run back to the chambers and do it again.

At four o'clock, the short, balding, and impeccably dressed Paul Ryan would enter and shoot his French cuffs, then he'd sit behind his personal electric typewriter by the window and tap out a daily column for the papers that did not subscribe to the more expensive blow-by-blow package. Around him was a humming, phone-ringing, noisy, news office. He would squint as smoke curled behind his silver-framed spectacles from the cigarette planted directly in the center of his lips. Unnoticed, the cigarette would drop ashes on his necktie and his white-on-white shirt, both from Louis of Boston on Tremont Street. He stared straight ahead, seeing nothing. He typed in slow, orderly spurts. He filled precisely two pages. By 4:45 p.m., I had the copy on the mimeograph machine. Before five o'clock, copies were inserted in a dozen envelopes, and I was on my way to South Station, to meet the conductor of the 5:30 p.m. South Shore express for Quincy, Brockton, Marshfield, New Bedford, and other points south. Most of the papers north of the city were weeklies, and they got their copies by mail.

By six o'clock most days, I was ready to make the late-copy run to Newspaper Row a few blocks away on Washington Street. I'd deliver to the *Globe*, the *Post*, the Associated Press and United Press, then around to Winthrop Square and Hearst's *Record*, the *American*, and the International News Service, finally back up to Tremont Street for a final stop at the *Herald* and *Traveler*, and then to the subway and home.

I was on deadline constantly, though I hardly knew the newspaper meaning of the word when I started this new life. I knew what a columnist was because my mother got the Republican *Boston Herald* each morning, and I sometimes read the contentious essays of pundit Bill Cunningham. (The *Herald's* State House reporter was a small, friendly guy named Eddie Devin.) On Sundays, we also got the middle-of-the-road *Boston Globe*. Now, I was surrounded by two dozen political reporters every day, people at the top of the food chain in Massachusetts journalism. I listened to their stories, their wisecracks, their boasting and complaining. I watched how each frowned or squinted, rubbed his forehead or chain-smoked, typed or talked into the phone, always on deadline. There was only one woman, a pretty brunette from the *Boston American* named Loretta McLaughlin. In those days, women reporters were called hens and covered soft society news or, the best of them, the courts. Women who covered hard news competed with the men by being hard-boiled. Loretta McLaughlin was the first I knew of a new breed. She had a confident smile and a courteous way, even with the lowly copyboy.

I also remember each of the men. One or two were imperious, several were cocky, and a few were so constantly preoccupied or distracted that they were difficult to approach. Several were friendly to me, and as my time in the State House went from months to years, a few became my mentors.

All of a sudden, government—*politics*—was not abstract or boring. It was about the officials I saw every day and how they ran things, helping some folks, hurting others, some taking much for themselves. In those days, the Massachusetts government was not completely on the level. Corruption had been a mainstay of many state governments and big city political machines. Boston and the Bay State long had been immersed in the struggle of the classes. The Irish and Italians were in political ascendancy; the founding Yankees in slow and stubborn retreat. The United States senators were two highborn patricians, Henry Cabot Lodge and John Fitzgerald Kennedy; neither of whom had apprenticed in city or state politics before heading for Washington. But the rest of the elected officials were mostly ethnics or Yankees who had paid their dues—Governor Paul A. Dever, Mayor John B. Hynes, Senate President John E. Powers, Massachusetts House Speaker Thomas P. O'Neill Jr., City Councilor Gabriel Francis Piemonte, Congressman Silvio Conte, City Councilor Joe Langone, future Governor Foster Furcolo. In my new setting, these names were part of every day. I still wasn't reading a newspaper or the copy I was carrying to newsrooms, but I could get some of the jokes and wisecracks in the pressroom, and I appreciated that I was moving among a brainy set. I had no sense, yet, that I could aspire to be one of them.

That spring, John came home from the seminary on vacation. I sat at the breakfast table with him, my mother in the background at the sink and the stove, and he told me I had to make plans. He informed me that the central plan was to take the entrance exam for Boston College the following year. It was a novel idea that I took to heart. Immediately, my grades markedly improved. I wrote to Boston College. I took the exam—before the days when you had to take the Scholastic Achievment Tests and before the days when you had to ace them if you wanted to get into Boston College. And in September 1952, I was a freshman.

12

Newspaper Days

By June, I owed Boston College $100 in tuition payments, and that began a four-year pattern. In September I would pay my overhanging debt and my next semester tuition. In the new year, I paid most of my second term tuition, and left the balance hanging until the next fall.

Through my contacts at the State House I got a full-time job that summer of 1953, working weekdays from 8:00 a.m. to 4:00 p.m. I was a copyboy at the *Boston American*, Hearst's earthy tabloid, which went to press five times a day with a new edition, and fought like hell with the *Boston Traveler* and the *Evening Globe* for a share of the audience of blue-collar Bostonians who read their news on the train home from work or with a beer before dinner.

This was to be my first test on the road to journalism. The *American* had a long history with some colorful chapters. In the '20s, its executive editor had favored wing-collar shirts, ascots, and cutaway coats, and visited the drawing rooms of Beacon Hill. By 1953, Hearst's Boston headquarters at 5 Winthrop Square was as worn out as the tenements, three-deckers, and taverns favored by our readers. The ornate exterior was stained with grime, the composing room a hodgepodge of aging linotypes and battered page forms, the subterranean presses ink-covered and beyond cleaning. Sometimes when Mayor Curley or his successors were piqued with Hearst's coverage, fire inspectors would be dispatched to 5 Winthrop Square, where they would exact fines and threaten a shutdown.

I worked in the third-floor city room, sitting with two other copyboys on a dark wooden bench against the wall until a rewrite man shouted "Copy!" or it was time for a coffee run. Sometimes I made up "books" of four half-sheets of scrap newsprint with three sheets of used carbon paper in between. These were stacked on the writers' desks and used to produce a single paragraph (or two, if the second was one short sentence). A copyboy was also stationed in front of the bank of teletypes, tearing off and sorting the Associated Press and United Press copy as the machines coughed them up, changing the paper rolls frequently, and at the sound of bells, tearing off a bulletin and running with it to the city editor.

Smoke curled up from almost every desk in the room, as if the clacking typewriters were smoldering. Ashtrays overflowed, were emptied, overflowed again. One copy boy was Jonathan Meigs IV, a blond-haired, prep-school innocent, perhaps fifteen. Another was older, a kid from Worcester named Tom Brady, who was living on his own and probably trying to write, although he never spoke of it. What I could gather was that he hated newspapers and newsmen because they had somehow hurt his family—in a tawdry domestic scandal, I imagined. He couldn't afford college but was tearing through books at the library, asking if I'd read Proust or Thomas Mann, among other authors I didn't know. Then there was the tough, sullen, and undependable young kid whose father, a man named Walter Howey, in his eighties with a glass eye, sat at a nearby editor's desk and read the paper, glowered, made a few phone calls, and left early with his son. Before coming to Boston to be with his newest wife and this youngest son, Walter Howey had been one of Chicago's most powerful editors; he'd run the infamous City News Bureau and the *Chicago Tribune* before he signed on with Hearst's *Examiner*. He was the model for the sour but loveable Walter Burns in Ben Hecht's play "The Front Page." (Hecht never found Howey loveable. He once said the editor "ripped the hearts out of reporters and stuffed them like olives." Hecht said you could tell Howey had a glass eye because "it was the warmer one.") One day on the bench, young Howey pulled out a large, menacing revolver. "This was John Dillinger's gun," he said.

The editor of the *American* was John Noonan—tall, beefy, florid-faced, white-haired and ill-mannered. At St. Ignatius Church in June, I watched him disrupt the funeral of Jack English, the elderly *American* political reporter.

Noonan talked throughout the eulogy, waving to dignitaries and pointing them out to a note-taking reporter, loudly making sure he had names for the second-day obituary.

—

I sat on the copyboys' bench and took in the process of creating a daily scandal sheet. We were expected to wear a dress shirt and a necktie, as did all the reporters and rewrite men and editors, including the legendary Walter Howey (although young Howey often forgot). Just the same, we were the blue-collar brawlers of Boston journalism. That summer, Noonan found his crusade—against higher fares on the subway. The Metropolitan Transit Authority had announced a coming fare increase to twenty-five cents and had limited the purchase of the then twenty-cent tokens to two per customer.

"Kid, wear a raincoat tomorrow," Noonan said to me one afternoon. The next day he handed me two dollars in dimes and sent me out to the five subway cashier kiosks within walking distance of Winthrop Square. At each one I stepped up to the window and bought two tokens. Just as I did, *bam!*, a flashbulb popped from the camera of the trailing *American* photographer. The next day's edition featured a double truck—the centerfold of the tabloid—exposing me as an unidentified token hoarder caught in the act exclusively by the *American*. I wish now that I had saved that double truck, but I was too embarrassed at the time.

Julius and Ethel Rosenberg were executed for espionage on June 19, 1953, the day after my eighteenth birthday—not much of a present from my country. Even then, long before the Soviet and American archives made it a certainty, many Americans believed Julius was a minor spy, not the man who gave the Russians the atom bomb, and Ethel was guilty of little more than loyalty to her husband. The Rosenbergs had two kids (made indelible by E. L. Doctorow's classic novel, *The Book of Daniel*), and people wondered about the patriotism of making them orphans. But the Hearst papers had no qualms. I sat on the bench the next day and read the eyewitness dispatch of Bob Considine, Hearst's star writer ("On the Line with Considine"), present at the execution. Of Ethel he wrote, "Her little minnow of a mouth was curled at the edges…She was looking straight ahead almost triumphantly" when they placed the hood. "As the torrent of electricity swept through her body…from every pore there seemed to emanate a strange, unearthly sound made up almost exclusively of the letter Z…A plume of smoke rose from her head toward the skylight."

Ethel wasn't dead. The attendants took off the straps and electrodes and the hood, checked her, found a pulse, strapped her and zapped her again, two jolts and again the plume of smoke. "She could relax now," Considine wrote, "her face possessed the same quizzical half-smile."

If this was journalism at its highest level, I wasn't interested.

Then came the young woman from the Boston suburbs who allegedly killed her ex-boyfriend's little sister in a fit of rage, then disappeared. Her story led the *American* each edition, from the day of the murder until well after she was picked up in Times Square, buying the Boston papers at the out-of-town newsstand. She was pretty. The *American* artists had airbrushed her high school yearbook picture so that she looked delicate and refined and belonging among the seraphim. Her ex was distraught. Her family was grieving. Her friends were puzzled. Police were baffled. What *really* happened?

And then one morning, I picked up the first edition and saw on the front "EXCLUSIVE! MILDRED'S OWN STORY: 'She was laughing at me. I stopped her.'" and inside on page three her byline. The article consisted of a bootlegged copy from the Boston police of her jailhouse confession. This was when the cops pretty much said and did what they wanted with suspects; a decade before the Earl Warren Supreme Court said if a citizen's constitutional rights were to mean anything, you had to tell them they didn't have to talk to cops without their lawyer present.

Late each afternoon, I would head up Summer Street past Jordan Marsh and Filene's, up Beacon Hill to the State House and the familiar precincts that not only offered steady income summer and winter, but a more refined view of journalism.

13

Penhallow Street

There is an Irish Catholic joke about the harried mother who went to confession and told the priest she was struggling to be patient and loving to her brood and often losing herself to anger if not despair. The priest counseled her to take the Blessed Mother as her model and to try harder. The woman glared through the confessional screen and replied, "Her and her one!"

The house on Penhallow Street became our home for many years. John was ordained and came home to St. Mark to say his first public Mass using the gold chalice that Mike Connolly had given him. Then he stood for hours in the parish hall, greeting family and friends and half the parish. They came in multitudes.

Donald came home from the navy, entered Newman Prep to complete high school, married Peggy McMasters from St. Peter's, moved to New Hampshire to work as a reporter at the Manchester *Union Leader,* and graduated from Saint Anselm's College. Peg and Don had two little boys and a girl. After newspapering at the *New Britain Herald* in Connecticut he went on to a Fortune 500 career and teaching at the college level.

Lou took her final vows and began a sixty-year-plus career as a Notre Dame nun, teaching and administering in schools across the diocese.

Catherine finished training at Boston City, married Don Muirhead, and had seven babies quickly, each time with a debilitating pregnancy that left her at times in hospital with tubes attached to her body and doctors fearful.

Every child thrived, and Cappy thrived in a nursing career in Boston and on the South Shore.

Anne finished high school and began a secretarial career in the archdiocese. She married Joe Kenney, had two boys followed by two girls, went to college at UMass Boston, and embarked upon a career as office manager, executive secretary, and publications editor at the Harvard University Institute of Politics.

I finished high school and Boston College, worked as a reporter at the Worcester *Telegram*, graduated from Naval Officer Candidate School, served three years on the destroyer *USS Purdy* as communications and combat information officer, then brought Ann Grady of Maplewood, New Jersey, home to Penhallow Street to meet Ma and Dad and announce our engagement. The story goes that when we left, Ma went to the phone and called one of my siblings. "The last of the nuts is getting married," she said. She then called Donald and told him he would be my best man, which was news to me and eliminated my dreams of an all-*Purdy* wedding party. The deck officer and the sonar officer were ushers, however. I had met Ann during my *USS Purdy* days when she was dating the Sonar Officer. We started writing, and it quickly became serious when she moved to Boston to get her Master's in education. She finished school and was teaching third grade in Bloomfield, New Jersey while I attended Columbia. We were married December 28, 1960 (The "Feast of the Holy Innocents" which well decribed Ann and me). The wedding was on a Wednesday during my semester break, and we set up housekeeping in a Glen Ridge, N.J. apartment. I graduated with honors from the Columbia University School of Journalism and joined *The Boston Globe*. Ann and I had two girls, and Ma became adviser and babysitter of last resort, as when Ann had an emergency appendectomy at Quincy City Hospital in the middle of the night.

Ma had had a phone installed as soon as we moved in at Penhallow, and she talked on it nonstop. One day in a mischievous mood, Dad came to the stairwell where the phone was kept and said to her, "Do you need hot soup?" as if she were a marathon swimmer.

Ann and I moved from Quincy to Arlington, and Dad came over to our rented duplex and, using Ann's drawing and dimensions, made a curved kitchen table that fit perfectly into a corner of that small room. Then he built a fence in the backyard to keep baby Kathy from falling down the steep bank to the driveway.

In 1962, when he turned seventy, he retired from the M. P. Horan Company, where he'd managed all the finished carpentry. The Horans had been loyal friends for 15 years but thought it was time for Dad to slow down. A week or so later, the doctors at New England Medical Center, around the corner from M. P. Horan and Company, who had seen Dad in their corridors for years doing carpentry, hired him to supervise their in-house construction work.

I was promoted to Washington Bureau Chief and, with financial help from the *Globe*, Ann and I bought a house in Bethesda, Maryland, that would be home for forty-six years. Dad and Ma came to visit, and when they left, we had a new room in the basement that we called "Papa's closet." Dad was 74. Once Papa's closet was finished, he stood on my cheap metal stepladder outside the kitchen window and affixed a thermometer ten feet above the ground. He had given Ann a small set of tools shortly after we married and said, with a twinkle in his eyes, "You'll need these."

The next year the doctors told Dad, then 75, he really should retire. He tried for a few months, but kept struggling through the help wanted ads. He applied for a night watchman's job at the Parker House Hotel. The manager looked at him and his work history and said, "You're no night watchman." He put Dad in charge of furniture repair and training young men to do light construction. His coworkers were immigrants from Latin America who had little English and no education. They had the same attitude toward Dad as most people—that he was a special man who knew much and shared all.

In March of 1970, Dad went off with his lunch in a bag to Shawmut Station to catch the subway to work, as he had done for more than fifty years. At work he had a heart attack and died in the arms of a young Latino apprentice whose baby son was Dad's godchild. The rescue squad took him the few blocks to Massachusetts General Hospital where Tom Durant, the deputy director, was waiting when Ma and my sister Cappy arrived. Tom and I had been riding around Cholon Vietnam two years earlier, in the midst of the Tet attacks, reminiscing about growing up on Samoset Street in Dorchester. Doctor Tom called me and said, "It was a great way to go. We should envy him."

The wake at Mulry's Funeral Home and the Mass were both filled with so many parishioners and good friends from our lives that it was an honor to be part of it. The pastor of Saint Mark, Father Donahue, had been a curate there for many years. His eulogy to "Joe" was quite personal and moving because he knew Dad so well.

Years later at some event a cousin I couldn't remember came up to me and said, "My God, you look so much like your father." And at a family reunion, one of my sisters looked at me and said to the others, "There goes Dad in L.L. Bean." Dad had more muscle, more patience and a lot more humility. But I do wear his face, and that makes me very happy.

Ma lived into her hundredth year. She enjoyed cooking for and teaching her grandchildren at Penhallow Street for many years after Dad passed away, until John got her into elderly housing. He came home from Latin America and waited hours on a bench at the housing authority until he got Ma a placement in a lovely subsidized unit in Dorchester Lower Mills by the old Baker's Chocolate factory. By then I was with the *Washington Evening Star* but still knew everyone in Boston politics. I was always too proud to ask a politician for a favor, or make the necessary phone calls, but if I had called Ted Kennedy's office, they would have handled the placement without a problem. When Dad died, Teddy had sent a handwritten note to Ma saying, *"I didn't know your husband, but Jim is a wonderful tribute to both you and your husband."*

John didn't ask for my help. Once before he had called me from La Paz to report that an American nun had been taken to a prison he knew well, which he said was sponsored if not owned by the Central Intelligence Agency. She was being tortured, he told me, and I should pressure the American government to rescue her. I was deeply conflicted and angry. I didn't cover Latin America or the State Department or the Central Intelligence Agency. I didn't have any verifiable facts. I would have been interfering simply because I could get attention. Fortunately I shared my angst and all the details with my desk mate at the *Star*, Jerry O'Leary. He was a marine colonel in the reserves, deeply conservative, and well connected in Washington, had covered Latin America and had a Latino wife.. He intervened with contacts at the State Department, and the nun was released.

John told me much later, he remembered some of the rough stories I had written in the past about the present mayor, Kevin White, and decided he would make the request through housing authority channels himself. He was kept waiting because the two women who ran the office were having a knock down-drag out fight. Finally he nailed the director sneaking out a side office door, and Ma got the exact apartment John wanted, in walking distance to St. Brendan's Catholic Church.

—

Ma's life had been getting easier for years. She flourished surrounded by her grandchildren who she took on forays into Boston to shop, to museums and to Mass at the crowded Arch Street Franciscan Chapel just off Washington Street. She visited friends who were housebound or in the hospital, stayed active in parish affairs, and used her phone to keep track of everyone. She was a prolific knitter, a loyal correspondent, and a recycler before that was fashionable. One would receive a greeting card that previously had been sent to her by someone, including perhaps Richard Cardinal Cushing whose every mailed plea for contributions was answered by Ma with five dollar bills. She sent one and all knitted gloves, hats and scarfs wrapped in great rolled up sections of the *Globe.* (She was indiscriminate about changing colors in the middle of a glove or hat or great woolen sock, but somehow the pairs seemed to match OK and her grandchildren wore them with smiles, love and good memories.)

She could be lonely and was standoffish in her new digs. Her growing family visited often though, and she could walk in the neighborhood and talk to the shopkeepers. (She became a regular at the liquor store.) One day one of the Muirhead grandchildren found her on the floor after a fall, unable to reach the phone. Cappy moved her into her overflowing home in Weymouth. Husband Don's sister had lived there, nursed by Cappy, until her death. Now Ma moved in, feisty as ever, cranky, and full of opinions for Don Muirhead. My Ann found Don one of her favorite in-laws, with a wonderful nature. We had all known him as a great guy, but now we discovered he was also a saint.

Cappy knew and had worked in the good nursing homes in Weymouth, and finally she placed Ma in the best, as a Medicaid patient. Ma lived there several more years, losing her memory and recognizing fewer and fewer visitors. She was not difficult, thanked the staff when they helped her and was pleasant to visitors, recognized or not. She had lots of visitors, and John and Lou each came constantly until she died peacefully in her hundred and first year. John had come home from Bolivia years before Ma started to fail. He had asked for an assignment to a parish where his Spanish language and long experience with the poor would be put to good use. He ended up in Brockton, where he got deeply involved with Catholic social workers organizing the poor. When Ma died, John was pastor of St. Peter's Church in Dorchester—a church designed and built as if a cathedral, but whose congregation had long since faded and now blended Irish with black, Cape Verdian, Latino, and Asian newcomers.

Ma's services were unique. The wake was a five-hour affair. The mourners included dozens of clergy who knew John or Ma or both, dozens of young college graduates who told me they worked with John, scores of St. Mark parishioners, and dozens of school chums of each of us from grammar school, high school, or college. One of my college friends drove his Porsche up from his mansion on Cape Cod. People from John's old Boston parishes came, as well as a large group of Vietnamese clergy and laypeople who said their special Vietnamese prayers for the dead. There were prayers in Spanish, decades of the rosary, and familiar prayers for the departed.

Whenever Ma went to a funeral—and she went to many-- she always counted the number of priests participating on the altar. At her funeral, the huge church was filled. The mostly black kids from the parish school were there with their nuns. The first three rows of the congregation were priests and nuns. And the altar area was crowded with monsignors and bishops. Cardinal John Law had a message read explaining that he was in Rome instead of in the Dorchester church praising the sainted mother of John Doyle.

Jimmy Muirhead, Cappy's youngest, was now in the funeral services business, and he handled the details. A flower car—an open-back limousine displaying all the wreaths and bouquets from the wake and funeral—followed the hearse. A police escort took us to the cemetery, and Boston police cars stopped traffic at the intersections.

One of the secondary eulogies summed up my mother. Her oldest grandchild, Mary Louise Muirhead, told the congregation about her adventures in Boston with Gram—how well Ma knew the subway system and how to get wherever she wanted to take you. She told how they would ride downtown, start at the Arch Street Chapel, hit Filene's Basement, the Boston Common, the Public Garden, and the Swan Boats. She said,

No matter what she chose to do, she did it with intensity, leaving a wide wake in her path. Gram could have been Margaret Thatcher or Madeleine

Albright or better yet, Eleanor Roosevelt. But she was my grandmother, a farm girl from Margaree who walked the streets of Boston like a queen, back straight, head held high.

Appendix

MacDonalds and Doyles in Cape Breton

THE MACDONALDS

The MacDonalds and the Doyles were part of the eternal migration of humans across the globe, seeking a better life in a better place. The MacDonalds came to Cape Breton in the 1770s. Calum MacDonald—Calum the Red-haired—was the first. He put his sick wife Catherine MacPherson, his twelve children, and his son-in-law Angus Kennedy on a transport ship in a sheltered cove along the Hebrides Islands off the western coast of the Scottish mainland. The story came down that as the family boarded the long boat and started toward the ship, the family dog plunged into the waves after them, her head cutting a V through the water, Calum shouting her back. But as she swam and swam and swam, Calum's threats turned to encouragement, until the dog came up on the stern, and Calum reached over and snatched her, taking her aboard the overcrowded ship and to the new land.

Catherine MacPherson died on the crossing, a victim of the fever, complicated by wormy food and brackish water. She was sewn into a canvas bag and dropped in the stormy North Atlantic. A week later, Angus Kennedy's wife gave birth to a baby girl named *Catriona na mara*, Catherine of the sea. The MacDonalds had embarked in August, and they reached the shore of Pictou, Nova Scotia, in early October. It is said that Calum the Red, who was then fifty-five, broke down and cried for two days. He had left Scotland a husband and arrived in Canada a widower, a grandfather, and the head of the MacDonalds in the New World.

His courage slipped. It would be two weeks before he could arrange for dories to take his clan across St. George's Bay to Port Hood and the waiting cousins who had land for them in this, the land of trees. In 1784, Cape Breton was constituted a British province. Calum walked more than a hundred miles from Cape Breton's west coast to the provincial capital at Sydney where he could receive the paper giving him title to his land. He was sixty years old then. He never remarried, though he lived to the age of 110. He saw his children, grandchildren, and great-grandchildren spread across the island, which was now annexed to Nova Scotia. He died in 1834, thirty-three years before Canada became a Confederation.

This is all recounted in a wonderful historical novel called *No Great Mischief*, written by a Cape Bretoner named Alistair MacLeod. The title is a quote from British General James Wolfe, who wiped out the Highlanders under Prince Charles Edward Stuart at Culloden Moor in northeast Scotland, on April 16, 1746. That ended the Jacobite uprising and Scottish independence. Wolfe went on to the French and Indian Wars, establishing British supremacy in Canada by defeating the French under General Louis Montcalm at Quebec in 1759. He won by recruiting his old enemies, the Scottish Highlander troops. He floated them down the St. Lawrence River in boats at night, forcing Montcalm into open battle on the Plains of Abraham. Wolfe wrote to his friend, British Captain Rickson, that the fierce highlanders were his secret weapon as well as his secret comfort: "no great mischief if they fall."

More MacDonalds came from the Hebrides in a steady flow, and my forebears were among them. In 1833, Alexander MacDonald, a schoolmaster from Arisaig, emigrated first to Antigonish on the mainland of Nova Scotia and then to Margaree, where he married Jane Gillis. The first of their nine children, John MacDonald, married Anne MacIsaac, whose father Angus had come to Upper Margaree from the Isle of Eigg in 1863. The second of John and Anne's seven was James MacDonald, my grandfather, who married Catherine Gillis at the church in Southwest. One of their children was my mother Catherine, who married my Dad, Donald Joseph Doyle, in Brookline, Massachusetts, on October 7, 1924.

—

THE DOYLES

Mabou Harbor, sixty miles southwest of the Margaree Valley, is where the two brothers, John and James Doyle, arrived from Wexford, Ireland, in the 1820s, well before Alexander MacDonald made his crossing from Scotland in 1833. When I visited the home where my dad was raised in nearby Glenora Falls, local folks told me the story—that the brothers swam to a ship in Wexford Harbor just before its departure for Cape Breton. I imagined my forebears as revolutionaries escaping the Black and Tan, the hated British troops. "Or they were horse thieves, just ahead of the constable," said a local with a wicked laugh.

My Dad wasn't much for family history, but we can discern much from the history of the Gaels. The Highland MacDonalds can trace their lineage back to Ranald, king of Dublin, Waterford, and York, who died in 921 AD. A hundred years before that, the Vikings had begun their raids on the northern coast of Scotland and the eastern coast of Ireland, marrying into the Celts of Ireland and Scotland.

In Gaelic, Doyle is *O'Dubhghaill,* or "dark stranger," a reference to the pre-Norman Vikings—Scandinavians—who settled Wexford and the surrounding coast. The name is the twelfth most common in Ireland, with some twenty-one thousand Doyles there today. James Warren Doyle was the militant Catholic bishop of Kildare early in the nineteenth century, and John Doyle, grandfather of Arthur Conan, was a painter in Dublin and the creator of political caricatures for *Punch,* the British satire magazine.

We don't know about the crossing of the Doyles to Cape Breton, except that it came a decade or more before the famine Irish who crossed to the New World enduring privations at least as bad as those that Calum the Red had met seventy years before. What the Doyles left was worse. Potato crops failed throughout Europe in 1845, and a million Irish died, paying with starvation, typhus, and cholera. Their grain and meat crops were exported to England as they lay dying. The British Conservative government declared what was happening to be an act of Divine Providence: the God of the High Anglican

Church was wiping out the papists. Americans raised relief ships, but much of that aid was squandered. The British declared that it would paralyze trade to give away food to the Irish. Cape Breton, this land of trees and rocky coast, fertile land and fruitful seas, was paradise to the few famine Irish who arrived there.

John and James Doyle escaped to northeast Mabou before the great hunger. James married Eleanor Murphy of Mabou, and their sixth-born was also James, who married Mary Beaton of Northeast Mabou. Their tenth child was Donald Joseph Doyle, my father, born February 4, 1892. He was orphaned at five years and taken out of school during second grade to help save the farm. He was illiterate as an adult. He worked building the railroads across Canada and the bridge in Halifax Harbor. He emigrated to Boston, where he married my mother in 1924.

Made in United States
North Haven, CT
29 November 2024

61146773R00064